HOW TO SURVIVE YOUR PARENTS

HOW TO SURVIVE YOUR PARENTS

by Roy Masters

Foundation of Human Understanding
P.O. Box 34036/8780 Venice Boulevard
Los Angeles, California 90034

HOW TO SURVIVE YOUR PARENTS
© 1982, 1987 by Roy Masters

Published by The Foundation of Human Understanding
Printed in the United States of America

For information, please direct your inquiry to:

For information, please direct your inquiry to:

The Foundation of Human Understanding
P.O. Box 1009
Grants Pass, OR 97526

Or call toll free: (800) 877-3227

Library of Congress Catalog Card Number 82-71162
ISBN 0-933900-10-4

Foreword

"Right on target! Roy Masters revitalizes ageless wisdom. For many, one hour with Roy Masters will be more beneficial than years of traditional insight psychotherapy."

Clancy D. MacKenzie
Director of Philadelphia
Psychiatric Consultation Service

"What a pleasure and an honor it is to endorse this book!

"I have had many years of training in the science of medicine. I have taught in universities and made contributions to medical literature and spent many years in private practice; then I heard Roy Masters' radio program. I must admit I was shocked at first, but I listened.

"Although some of his statements appear contradictory to traditional scientific beliefs, I sensed an underlying ring of Truth. I was intrigued and sent for the literature.

"I was astounded to find how right-on his principles were and how they filled in the gap I had always felt was missing in modern medicine. Today's fundamental misconception that science is the Truth is clearly rectified by what Roy Masters teaches.

"The Foundation of Human Understanding has been a great help to me in my work with many difficult problem patients.

"I must warn you, however, this book is not for everyone."

Albert R. MacKenzie, M.D.

"*...I must say, on the basis of a year's experience, that the application of this technique has made a significant contribution to the treatment of the great majority of those people who have learned it. Particularly gratifying has been the experience with those individuals, actually quite numerous, who do not seem to benefit from classical analytically oriented psychotherapy, but who through the process of meditation do begin to develop insight into their difficulties and thereby a new sense of control over their lives.*

"*In closing I would like to add a personal note of thanks to Roy Masters for his generosity and encouragement in the application of his techniques to medical practice.*"

George M. Hayter, M.D.

"*Children are imprinted by the personality of the dominant parent at an early age, and they will show the same behavior subconsciously in their later lives toward their own children and spouse. People unknowingly set themselves up to reproduce the trauma of their earlier lives and thus imprint their own children and pass their problem on from generation to generation.*

"*By using the meditation technique as taught by Roy Masters, the individual can overcome his problem by becoming objective and by understanding it, and therefore is able to overcome his compulsive tendency to respond to the world around him, to his spouse, and to his own children in the manner of the past generation.*"

Irene A. Royko, M.D.

"*As a pediatrician I believe that as a parent you are potentially more dangerous to your own child than are any germs. If your child is having physical or emotional problems, it is a signal to you that you are doing something wrong. Most parents would rather blame vitamins, diet, the weather or the stars for their childrens' problems. Some parents intuitively feel responsible for their childrens' problems but can't see clearly where their failing lies. If you want to learn how to truly love your children (that is, protect them from harm, both from yourself as well as from others) then I prescribe the "medicine" in Roy Masters' book,* How To Survive Your Parents.*"

Richard Mittleman, M.D.

Contents

1: Hate Your Parents, Hurt Your Kids

Let's face the facts and take a good, hard look at where all your troubles began—in your home! The great majority of parents are completely deranged, if not criminally insane. At the very least, they have a streak of madness in them a mile long. For the most part, parents are impossible, confusing, dangerous creatures with whom to deal. There is only one cure, which, if it doesn't help your parents, will at least help *you*. That cure is love.

Love is what most parents need more than anything in this world. They were never given love when they were young, because *their* parents didn't have any to give. In fact, the present miserable, loveless state of humanity can be traced all the way back to antiquity, to the original failing of a man to extend a correcting love toward a woman. Adam might have said, "Eve, don't tempt. Be a good girl and put that apple down." But he didn't. One man's failing resulted in mankind being born under the tyranny of unloved and unloving authorities. We are infected with fear, hate and madness from the day we are born. There is no escape except through love. But because no one has real love to give, we are hurt and confused about what love is.

It seems strange to say that children need to love their parents, because tradition has it the other way around. But what if the love from which children need to draw is nowhere to be found? Then, maturing to the role of parents ourselves, what are we to do? Are we doomed forever because we have never known love and therefore cannot give it? Of course not! The truth is that the love you are seeking comes more from loving others than from being loved yourself. It must be the kind of love that does not *expect* to be loved in return.

Ninety-nine and nine-tenths per cent of all your parents were emotionally crippled in their formative years. They had violent or impatient parents who "laid a trip" on them which rendered them incapable of extending love to their children. The emotional traumas of childhood not only psychologically blocked your parents' ability to love you, but also compelled them to pass a kind of mental burden on to you. They have been driven to set you upon a path from which all your problems arise: problems with your parents, yourself, your own family and with all the world. You are so caught up in your mind with the struggle that you now find yourself behaving just as inhumanly toward your offspring as your parents did to you, and their parents did to them.

How could your parents not be impatient? How could they not be resentful? Violence is all they have ever known, just as impatience is all your children will know from you unless you awaken.

We, the unloved, are all born under an ancient hypnotic curse. The Bible tells us that the sins (failures) of the fathers are projected to the third and fourth generations, but His mercy is extended to those thousands who yearn for God and keep His laws. The Creator's law is love. His love is not the kind you get by wanting it from people; neither is it the supportive kind of love you give in order to get people to love you in return. It is much more profound than that.

The conflict you feel raging within you and within your own family began with your reaction to some kind of traumatic parental tease or pressure. No matter how hard you try to compensate for the harm your parents did by emotionalizing you, you cannot help being the impatient, cruel extension of their nature. Whether you are hurting from being hated or from being corrupted through spoiling love, you are under a compulsion to pass emotional and psychological confusion on to succeeding generations.

The world is mad—or haven't you noticed?

Everyone you meet on your journey through life is mad in his or her own unique style. The formula for dealing with every twisted personality quirk in people is the same as that for dealing with your parents. If you can't deal with your parents properly, you become progressively unable to cope with anyone or anything else. Sooner or later you feel the full effect of the curse. You will fail, blame your parents and hurt your own children. Perhaps you will knock them down to build yourself up, or build their egos up to bolster your own ailing pride, taking credit for what you have motivated them to do. You always play a role! You are the one who gets hurt, and then you become the one who does the hurting.

Patience is the way to perfect love. By not responding to a parental tease, you express correcting love, which lifts you out of the age-old system of chain-reaction response. Patience is love for children, as well as for parents. Patience is love for mankind.

Patience is the evidence of love maturing, and it is this kind of unselfish love which points the way to maturity for those around you. So, you see, filial love, parental love and brotherly love should all reduce to the one *agape*, Godly love—patience.

May the Creator bless you to see that your parents are out of control, that something in them is driving them to hurt you. If you are able to see this clearly, you will not feel the hurt or the need to relieve your pain by hurting others. You will also feel relief in realizing that you are not mad for seeing what is wrong with them. With compassion comes patience and, through patience, the good which overcomes evil.

A soul inclined toward good, will see clearly that it has no alternative except to be patient. It is not a matter of conscious control, but of being so close to reality—so objective, so distant to emotion—that you become part of the solution rather than part of the problem.

Patience is the gift of the Spirit, given through understanding. Understanding the spiritual agony others suffer in their cruelty toward you will help you have compassion for them, rather than feelings of resentment. You will no longer feel such hatred or cry so many tears.

Patience is the perfect offense and the perfect defense. With patience to sustain you under trial, the unholy spirit which drives your parents cannot get through you to hurt others ever again. Your patience can free even those who try to hurt you with their impatience.

Parents are like oversized kids who have never outgrown their selfishness. Your patience is the love which might help them to see that. Regardless of whether they ever see it or not, your patience will keep *you* safe from the sick, unspeakable thing that has made a home in them. The naughty, love-starved child (in you) is corrected each moment you stand firm with patience. Each precious moment in which you give to others the patient love that you would have them give to you, you will find welling up in yourself the substance of good for which you have always hungered.

Slowly but surely you will be set free from the mental torment of getting either too much attention or not enough. When you do not reach out for the love of the world, when you begin instead to have compassion, God rewards you with the infilling warmth of His friendship. You see, seeking the ego-supporting affection of the world has made you an enemy of God.

When my father died, I cried. I missed him. There was an emptiness in my life; I couldn't believe he was gone. In futility, I sought him in other people. Then one day a profound thought occurred to me that saved me from sadness: *the man who died was not my real father.* God is my only true father. It was He who revealed this truth to me; believing in it comforted my soul, and I have been growing in His truth ever since.

The ultimate purpose of love is to correct another's ego-needs and cravings, to set him free from the need of personal and social ego-support. All of us must eventually find our own ground of being. We must be strong from within. Paul said that the more I love (correct) you, the less you love (need) me.

If you are to survive the holocaust of life and receive the prize of salvation, you must deal with unreasonable pressures in a reasonable way—that is, with patience, from the ground of your inner being. Without patience for others, you cannot be patient with your own inherited faults (sins), or those which have slipped in through the sin of impatience.

Are you stubborn in your pride? Then you will be stubborn in the belief that you must have love from the world, because your guilt makes you a desperado, demanding sympathy and affection. Don't harden your heart, or then you will be unable to believe the truth, and that unfortunate state will set you more firmly upon the path of futility, until your torment finally awakens you (if you let it).

Just as impatience is the primitive energy of pride, so is patience the force behind humility.

Because of their proclivity toward pride, people can be tempted by cruelty to be impatient and resentful. Impatience tempted and trained you to be resentful as a child and so reinforced the nature of pride, which now feeds impatiently on the reactions of your own resentful, fearful victims. Just as resentment toward parental impatience made you the inferior projection of the wickedness lurking in them, now as a parent yourself you find you are pulling rank in the same miserable chain-gang of command.

Perhaps you can realize what love is, if only by observing what you have suffered from its lack. Upon reaching maturity, you find yourself at the threshold of understanding—but it is a negative experience; whereas, if your parents had known how to love you, it might have cultivated your relationship with truth in a positive way. If your parents had loved you as they should have—patiently, with a firm, no-nonsense approach—they might have stopped the error growing inside you dead in its tracks. Through the persistence of their patience, you could have eventually felt their divine concern toward you. Loving the good in them, you would have matured toward the origin of goodness to become a friend of God. Unfortunately, you have grown so corrupt that your conscience now seems to be the enemy. Your present resentment toward the "enemy" makes it impossible to take that one step beyond resentment to peace and freedom from sin.

Even if your parents had been perfect, you might have hated them just the same for not letting you have your own way. Through their long-suffering (not hating you back), you would have been privileged to feel the redeeming shame of your own conscience. Instead, you now feel only the pain of conflict, accompanied by a need to escape from reality into the false redemption of pleasure, resentment and blame. The trick you are using is this: if everything wrong is all *their* fault, it follows that there is no fault in you!

Resentment, bitterness and blame, supported by a *real* reason, can sustain a judgment. In other words, you tend to fixate on other people as the cause of your problems to avoid seeing the manifestations of error in yourself. If your parents had been patient, it would have pulled the rug from under you and made you face yourself, for your judgment would have been without a cause. We all owe our children the opportunity to experience "judgment-without-a-cause."

If you hadn't resented your own awakening, you might have been shamed into reconciliation with your conscience, and conscience would have become your friend. It is this sort of inner contact which causes men to share with one another the greater life and wisdom of their Creator.

Beware of trying to figure out what makes people act the way they do. Fall into this trap and you will become as mad as they are! It is sufficient to realize that there is something eating your parents' minds away from the inside and trying its damnedest to make a new home in you.

See it, know it and never doubt it. Be objective. Have compassion and, above all, be patient. *Hate the sin by not hating its victim, the sinner.*

Hold fast to the faith. Respond only with patience and your innocence will be preserved. Old guilts, fears and shortcomings will bubble up to the light to be resolved and you will find then that you can be patient with yourself.

A knowledge of the whys and wherefores of cruel or unnatural behavior is not what you need—not to begin with, anyway. What you need more than anything is patience, patience that comes from seeing clearly and not doubting what is revealed.

Patience is the foundation and heartbeat of the new being. Impatience has built the problem-personality, but patience will tear down the sin-self and make way for the salvation of the Lord.

Impatience is strong before the weak and weak before the strong. The unholy response to impatience is resentment, wherein the victim swells up in judgment and also in conflict with the Divine Will.

Resolving your resentment and impatience is the key to just about every problem you have, mental, emotional and physical.

Address yourself to the weaknesses of resentment and impatience, and all other symptoms which have grown out of them will disappear. For example, if your over-weight problem comes from being upset, then you must address yourself to the upset before the overeating problem can be truly overcome.

An impatient person's need for judgment-food can project as violence in his or her children. Through resentment, the beast of pride grows and uses impatience to have its prideful way with the weak. Impatience projects, while resentment has a way of accepting what is projected. Impatience thrives on hurting and resentment thrives on being hurt. A good example of this is the complaining, resentful wife who secretly thrives on the judgment she feels toward the violent and cruel husband whom she has cultivated to take liberties with her.

Fail to cope with impatience patiently *just one time* and you will become a permanent victim. What is set up is a psychological treadmill of morbid thinking, feeling and compensating that sustains the wickedness of others then projects misery and suffering without end.

You may try to cope with unreasonable people but, without the virtue of patience, their temptation proves too much for you. Your soul's failing emerges as resentment, which becomes violence, suppressed or expressed.

The guilt of your failing causes you to hide from reality in the jungle of your thoughts. You become a fearful psychotic, a people-pleaser who is subject to all manner of wicked authorities. Or you try to overcome your fear of authority by evolving to *become* that authority. You are no longer the one who gets ulcers—you become the one who gives them.

Being lost in your emotions and thoughts is what allows the harm of hell to come through. The prideful nature in parents projects problems through the children's egos and then refuses to see where those problems originated.

Children often carry a heavy burden of blame all their lives. They learn to take the blame themselves or, as their parents did to them, they compel others to take up their guilts in order to relieve their own burden. However, it never works. In the process of struggling to accomplish either one of these wretched ends, they only accumulate more guilt that further addicts them to the guilty process of blaming and accepting blame.

We carry complexes, strange suggestions, guilts, fears and inferiorities which loveless authorities have pressed into our heads. It is only natural to feel that love can cure them, because it could, if only we knew exactly for what we should be looking.

Deprived of this elusive love, you have developed into a very guilty, selfish person indeed—much worse than just a little child who couldn't grow up. The conscience you now feel exists not only because of the pain of not being loved and corrected, but also because of the sin of pride which has slipped in through resentment. Through judgment and blame, the sin-nature continues to mushroom in you. Resentment, impatience and blame have become part of a cycle of accepting sin and projecting it.

Resentment cheats you of love. Resentment is the classic response to temptation. It is this which deprives you of life and substance and makes you into a nothing which tries desperately to be a something. More determined (and more willful) than ever, you begin manipulating for love. Alas, you end up being manipulated through your own maneuvering. Your efforts backfire and make you ever more resentful. For example, you are so ambitious for approval that you can become too obliging, the idea being that others will be obligated to give you love. All this does is give people the power to take advantage of you which, in turn, makes you angry and causes the pain that compels you to try harder to get approval. Perhaps you will try to be perfect so as to be worthy of love, but this sham of perfection often frightens people off and leads to another rejection.

The love you need can never come, as you foolishly think it will, through people-pleasing. Furthermore, you can no more make people love you, when you have resentment toward them, than your parents could straighten you out by resenting and being impatient with you.

How could your parents not be impatient? How could they not be resentful? Violence is all they have ever known, just as impatience is all your children will ever know from you unless you awaken.

At best you will only receive something that *looks* like love, which your impatience sometimes obliges people to give you. Their hostile reaction to you makes them feel guilty and that can cause them to seek your approval to assuage the guilt. Approval, whether from them or for them, is destructive. Approval is never a corrective form of love. This kind of closeness is a spoiling, supporting love for everything that is secretly wrong with both of you.

Approval reinforces error, which in turn breeds dependence. Contempt and resentment grow from that dependence because your dependence is evidence that neither one of you has enough real love to set the other free. Resentment is what leads back to dependence on the love which enslaves, and a vicious cycle is formed which leads from "love" to hate and back again.

Through impatience and resentment you lose understanding as a positive, constructive force, and gain it back in the negative form of a guilty conscience. This is the pain you are foolishly trying to resolve through supporting and being supported by others.

Let me remind you again that one can only experience true love and real gain through patience; failing that, you experience only sin and loss. Therefore, be patient with the cruelty and treachery, the greeds and needs of others; then you can be patient with your own shortcomings. *Patience cures everything.* Any feeling of loss or inferiority, of becoming a "nothing" while striving to be a "something," is caused by your hostile response to impatient authority.

Patience will help one transcend sin and mortal weakness, beginning with the infantile ego-need for mother's love and ending with the sexual love for mother-wife.

Remember those two forms of love. One kind of love is worldly, supportive of and sympathetic to the failing of pride, plus all the sickness symptoms which have wormed their way into you through resentment. The other, *true* love is divine. It is made manifest as patience, which rebukes sin and disease (the symptom of sin).

Patient admonishment is all you will ever need. The fulfillment of patience is God's reward in you for not looking to the world for love to comfort your pride.

Patience works as a creative power, whether others are patient with you or you are patient with them. There is benefit to both parties, whether it is you who appreciates the patience and so receives the good, or whether it is you who is being patient.

A baby requires the warm body and the ego-comforting, ego-supporting love of mother. But too much affection is a deadly temptation to the ego of the child and can weaken its personality.

Seeing to it that the child transcends his need for mother's enslaving love is the father's job. A father must have special power to wean his child away from a female-centered existence and cultivate in him an independent and God-centered life. Unfortunately, most men are like drunks, addicted to the nectar of female love. They are insecure, pathetic, selfish creatures who wallow in the reassurance they get from making mothers out of wives. These selfish sons of witches are impotent as far as true love is concerned.

Mother's affection, without the overriding, *corrective* influence of a father's firm, no-nonsense, patient presence, tends to build the child's ego-identity beyond its natural state and, by so doing, unwittingly tempts the child to become spoiled and prideful. Escaping guilt through a sense of power is the usual motive for spoiling a child. Getting high on the worship you require is an attempt to make good the loss and pain you formerly experienced at the hands of your hateful parents. The sin which has made you a loser now impatiently cries out for its own victim to feed upon.

Mother's love is a selfish, ego-supporting, crippling need-to-be-needed that can only tempt, so that her own ego will in turn be supported by a weak, obedient, psychotic victim. This love is *always* destructive. It can never correct. It will no more correct the child's ego-need than bartenders or dope pushers will correct their victims' needs. Behind *every* need-to-be-needed is a victim seeking someone to victimize.

The vampires who seek to possess may bring about their own rejection. When rejection causes resentment, the impatient vampire becomes the resentful victim and everything turns around.

Because selfish love always hurts (both to give and to receive), it always metamorphoses into resentment. Just as resentment addicts us to needing, impatience addicts us to being needed. So it comes to pass that we hate what we need and need what we hate. Psychology calls this contradictory condition "ambivalence," because psychology doesn't differentiate between need and love. One cannot love and hate at the same time, simply because true love transcends hate. But you can hate and *need* at the same time! Notice how "love" is purposely confused with need. The prideful cannot admit that theirs is the wrong kind of love—it has to be the only love there is.

Loving and being loved, hating and being hated; your whole life revolves around sin. When sin grows up inside you and starts to hurt (conflict), it cries out for comfort—sympathy and "understanding" for what it is. While some people enjoy controlling you through frustrating that need, others simply can't resist rising to the occasion to comfort you, like angels from heaven (and controlling you that way).

For this reason, no woman in her wrong mind, craving "love" herself, will correct a child—she wouldn't do it even if she had the power. She will impatiently cripple and spoil her child for what her tormented soul craves. Often she rejects her baby for demanding something from her, something she herself wants from him. In her wrath, she teases and terrorizes the child to worship her and rewards its weakness with false affection. A female child may grow up to be like mother; the male child will seek a mother. And that is the hell into which we were all born.

A noble child or husband cannot and will not provide the feedback of worship, but they are called "cold," "unfriendly" and other uncomplimentary names. The attention-seeking witch has little tolerance for anyone's need but her own, and she is threatened by those whom she cannot destroy to feed her ego's need.

Were you resentful at being rejected? If so, that was where the spirit of your mother succeeded in getting inside and making you a loser—a nothing trying to be a something. To this day, everyone who accepts you uses you just as your mother did. You bow and scrape, hoping upon hope to get approval, but all you do is give your guts for tidbits, pats on the head. You are locked into this stupid mistake over and over again. You are under a compulsion, a hypnotic spell. Eventually, you may be driven to be cruel to get "by crook" what you can't get "by hook."

And there you go again, hurt becomes resentment and resentment changes to guilt. The pain of guilt whets your need, or your need-to-be-needed, and the world calls it "love." Behind this kind of love is resentment.

Now do you see why you are so frustrated, angry and riddled-through with problems? Your soul, needing divine love, has made the classic error of seeking supporting love *for* the original sin-self rather than reproving love which would correct you *from* the ways of pride. You need to be chastened from this unholy need. You need to be corrected. Only the serpent will love you as you are.

It is common for a woman to mistake a bully's power for the manly strength she needs in a husband. Such women-corrupted men delight in putting women down, trying to get back what they lost to their mothers.

Gentlemen, it is too late for you to seek the salvation of a warm body. You are beyond the point where momma's reassurance would have a value. Look! Underneath every need for sexual reassurance is that other ego-need for momma's body-love for baby. Wean yourself away from both these needs, before you make a mother out of your wife. Destroy your woman with your selfish, infantile need and she will destroy you with her "love."

Resentment is the key. Needful love, whether fulfilled or frustrated, takes more than it gives. Contempt goes to the winner, resentment to the loser, while guilt accumulates to both of you. And what does guilt do when we won't face our faults? It drives us to "love" with need and with the need to be needed.

Indeed, any guilt you may presently feel in relation to your parents can cause you to take the blame for whatever happens to them. Let us say, for example, that your father was a drunk and you resented him. In this case, you could be compelled to feel that what happens to him is all your fault for not giving him the love he wanted from you, for not being the "good" dutiful child. Perhaps you have been nagged with the notorious line, "You will be the death of me yet!" Granted, you may well be a problem child, but only because of your parents' impatience, cruelty and seductive "loving." But parents have the power to slyly turn it around the other way, to lay all the burden of their sickness and tragedy on you. God! How you resented that! *It was through your own resentment that the burden was laid upon you.*

Think of it! The guilt you feel as a result of your

resentment at being rejected can be turned around so that you accept responsibility for your parents' sickness and failure. Guilt (through the emotion of resentment) now compels you to give your guts for your parents' approval. But no matter how good you are to them, you can never make them happy. Everything you do makes them more miserable, for which they blame you! Indeed, some of the blame *is* yours—you are making them worse by giving them sympathy instead of compassion, which is corrective.

Like an alcoholic dreams of drink, so have you dreamed of love. You have been high on love and high on rejection. You are like a gambler, always challenged to get even with the house, but losing to it again and again. At long last, when you can no longer pay up, you get your legs broken to satisfy the debt. There is no end to what you have to give in order to get, and all you get is got! Just like the gambler, once you lose, the loss challenges, fixates and fascinates you (resentfully) to win, if only to prove you can beat the system, even if you lose your soul. It's all you nothings have left to trade for becoming somethings.

The bottom line is this: the basis of all sin lies in *being deceived*. So when your sinning ego keeps wanting the glorifying, sustaining, justifying "love" that you have been (deceived into) wanting, you must keep sinning and struggling to get back what you have lost in the deception.

Frustration always arises when you *will* into being that which you think is important. As soon as you welcome the truth—which is that you shouldn't need worldly love —your anxieties will begin to disappear. Not only will anxiety vanish, as understanding neutralizes the frustration of reaching in the wrong direction, but, going deeper, understanding will also take away all the resentment, blame and emotional needs which masquerade as love.

2: Parental Injustice: The Cause of Violence

Crime, delinquency and mental illness, although rooted in individual willfulness and ambition, are actually planted and nurtured by culture. This is precisely the reason why nations cannot solve any of their problems. The stubborn pride of man traditionally points at the symptoms of sickness (which are the result of corrupting cultural influences) and labels *them* the disease itself.

Traditionally, parents tend to blame their problem children rather than admit that the offspring are projections of their own troubled selves. Parental help is rejected by troubled children because parents are the root-cause of the problem, and their "help" only drives children deeper into a psychotic state.

Let's get straight to the heart of the principal cause behind national and family strife: People become dehumanized through the very weaknesses which culture promotes, namely, national pride, sexual pride and the pride of ambition. The effect of ego-reinforcement which we derive from effort, from striving and from pushing, actually reverses the positive effects we are trying to achieve. The harder one tries to "make it big" for oneself and family, the worse off everyone becomes.

Once we become infected with the spirit of pride and begin striving for superiority, we actually become inferior creatures of habit, responsive to motivators who literally consume our substance while glorying in both our successes and failures. The pain of our loss at the hands of a motivator compels us to become destructive, to apply degrading pressure to others, especially to our families.

Pride is very arrogant and defensive regarding its culturally implanted imperfections. This being the case, it follows that the error of your way is almost undetectable (to you, at least). The next time your beloved son comes home high on something or other, notice how in *his eyes* *you* will seem to be the bad guy for observing his errant behavior. Not surprisingly, children have a special appreciation for their buddies who do not see their wrongs, just as you parents have your entourage of friends (fiends, really) who accept you as you are. You may see your children's faults, and they may see yours, but you rarely see your *own* mistakes, because you are all too fixated on one another's evils and too busy judging to discern your own faults.

Sensuality and an unreasoning psychology evolve out of the fall from grace to pride. Wherever you find pride, there too will you find many uncontrollable lusts, attended by a host of sympathetic, exploiting, friendly fiends, sucking and nourishing themselves on the dying by seeming to worship those contemptible weaknesses.

When we are lost in any successful appeal to our pride, we awaken amid a world of sensuality. If our self-consciousness does not become repentance, the condition worsens and terrible fears, anxieties and guilts develop.

Primitive desires are awakened by the tempter, who then accepts the degenerating creature-self as the real man. The reason for re-emphasizing this point is to impress upon you the fact that, in order to have the authority to correct the evolving beast of pride in your children, you yourself must be in the process of outgrowing your own childish pride and sensuality. Failing that, your very presence tempts your children to misbehave. And when they fall to that temptation, their vile ways tempt you to be even more self-righteous and judgmental.

Pride causes some people to try to compensate for their secret shame, while others pridefully flaunt their shameful nature. Those who conceal their sins form the main body of pretentious social climbers and hypocritical achievers. Save for a minority of seekers and finders, humanity is made up of drop-outs, criminals and low-life degenerates.

You must realize that any imperfection of the ego (pride), no matter how nobly camouflaged, tempts others. The inherent wickedness of your pride, draped in false piety, is constantly tempting your children to become prideful, sensual animals just like you—animals who cover up and suppress their evolving desires, or animals who openly and "honestly" express their contempt and vileness. The latter, comparing themselves with your phoniness (as you compare yourself with their wickedness), see themselves as being more honest because of their lack of pretense about being the weirdos, perverts, crooks or degenerate animals you have made them.

The default of virtue, by its very nature, presents an irresistible tease which provokes others to become beasts or hypocrites just like you. You parents shape the destiny of your children in their formative years. You set them up for conflict and tragedy. Then the educational system adds its share of cruelty. Friends and lovers tempt, too. As we grow older and more degenerate, we fall into the clutches of medicine men and welfare workers who ensure our final demise. When society has finished all its deadly work, the scene is like a battleground strewn with the dead and wounded, with field hospitals for alcoholics and battered wives, with hot lines for the suicidal, and with murderers, rapists, thieves and drug addicts lurking deep in the trenches. Madness and horror are rampant as far as the eye can see.

Where the appeal to the ego (or pressure or cruelty) finds its mark, death enters, preceded by dehumanizing spiritual, psychological and physical changes. We are never better off, or more superior, as we thought we would be when we fell for the lying promise inherent in every ego-appeal.

Teach, tempt or challenge any child to be prideful and you set the stage for his ultimate destruction. It takes about twenty years of hard work to destroy a child's mind, and to succeed one must work steadily at it. That destructive handiwork starts the day a child comes into the world. Compulsive parents, lacking the redeeming quality of humility which would teach them love, cannot rest until their murderous work is done and the only "rest" they find then is in the grave.

Through cruel, inhuman pressure, often disguised as loving concern for his well-being and success, the real spirit of a child is slaughtered, and something awakens which is unholy standing in the place of the holy—an inferior creature full of fear and guilt, dependent on its corrupters for lying reassurances and motivation, even when that motivation is hate. From this point on, the corrupted soul needs a corrupt external model to inspire ("out-spire," really) the growth of the newly-implanted identity. You and your conformist children have your culture, and your rebels have their counter-culture motivators.

When you see your children following the wrong crowd, realize that it is because your hypocrisy has excited in them a spirit of prideful rebellion. Your rebel offspring is on the outside what *you are really like inside.* Your child may not know it because he is trying so hard not to be like you but, like it or not, he is really a projection, a mirror image, of your secret life of failure and sin.

That evil, which you fail to see in yourself (but which you see in your kids), came by way of your parents' failure and the failure of fathers ever since the fall of Adam to Eve and of Eve to the serpent of temptation. *You are what motivates you.* You have merely covered your evolving impieties with religiosity, hard work, medicine, drugs, alcohol, and with a whole smorgasbord of social pacifiers.

You might well ask, "How do I regain that original innocence?" The answer is that you cannot, unless you come to understand the mysteries of pride and deception. *You must yearn to know the purpose for which you were created.* Then, and only then, will you see the mystery of how pride ushers in your personal downfall, as well as the destruction of your family, of nations and of the world.

Those who fall to and are ruled by deception also learn to rule others through it. Most people are dependent upon deception in one form or another for everything they are and everything they have. The conforming child will cling to the lying love of parental deception, while the rebel child will cling to scum (who have the same lying nature you can't see in yourself) for their reassurances.

Rebels have their Fuhrers, hypocrites have their presidents, and the intrigue between the rebels and the squares keeps hell on earth alive, evolving to power through the warring factions.

Developing a hard survival-shell is the way every ego protects implanted sin. As an extension of the wrong, the corrupted soul defends the indwelling sin against observation. We feel wrong when we are exposed, so we think that those who make us feel bad are cruel and unkind. Like criminals running from the law, we slink into the dark theater of our minds for the velvety companionship of shady friends.

Right there you have the reason why the ruling class of seducers and corrupters has so much going for it and why it is so easy for both underworld and overworld tyrants to create legions of loyal "patriots," drug addicts, criminals, perverts and revolutionaries. Your ruined children are drawn magnetically to various forms of corruption because they need cultural reinforcements for the pride which their parents have inculcated into them through mindless, cruel or neglectful ways.

In this vast social con-game, every egotist, as he is "taken," assumes the identity of his god, the taker. Then running from his shame, striving to feel more and more omnipotent, he learns to steal. Stealing may not be wrong to him, because it fills the ego-need to feel good, like God. It feels like he is only taking what rightfully belongs to him, the king! (For this, and for many other reasons of pride, the world admires takers more than givers.) The pattern is for the taken to become the taker, just as the person who has been bitten by the vampire soon becomes a vampire himself. Every ego is infected and fascinated with the lie which makes him feel as good as God, and this need gets worse as it is gratified because the guilt increases.

To be "promoted" to the rank of a taker, "king wrong" and deceiver, one must first allow oneself to be taken (fall to temptation). That is why your child's misguided ego does not mind being taken in by his wicked friends and phony gurus. As he surrenders himself, the victim earns the right (through sacrifice) to be fashioned in the likeness of the taker. A mysterious psychic change occurs in your child as he is corrupted—with each encounter, he becomes a little more like his source. If he surrenders himself completely, "unselfishly," (as kids do with friends and various cults), he receives an illusion of perfection as he becomes one with his "god." So it comes to pass that he learns to turn slavery into a glorious achievement; descending is seen as ascending to glory. It is his giving in to parental pressure to avoid arguments, his being rewarded for weakness with a brownie button of approval, that has set the stage for this sort of thing to happen.

From the moment your child is first taken in, he will give his all to his parasitical cult leader or lover. He will beg for alms in the streets, cheat his clients and customers and turn everything over to his bloodsucking mentor who rewards every weakness as a religious virtue. All sinners worship and identify with idols in order to become the object of worship themselves. (Careful, you enshrined mothers; your sons could become homosexual in this fashion.)

One moment your child can seem to be a decent, family-centered, home-loving kid; and the next, he is the enemy. All your efforts to reform him—your ultimatums, your pleading, your being kind one moment and cruel the next—only refuel his rebellion, making all the ego-reinforcing pleasures of sin more alluring.

As long as your pride stands in the way, you can never correct children; that is an impossible feat. You can try being nice and try being mean, but nothing works. The absence of divine authority in you merely increases the pain of conflict in your children and whets their desire for the very things you forbid, hardening your rebel offspring and increasing their appetite for ego-soothing drugs, crime and degenerate, supportive friends.

If I were the devil, one role in which you would find me (other than extolling the pleasures of sin) is that of zealously pressuring and exhorting others to virtue. Some, sensing where I was coming from, would reject the values I was teaching, thinking that they were thereby rejecting the wickedness of hypocrisy. That is just one of the ways I would trick them into finally accepting evil as good. Between the blind acceptance and the resentful rejection of the phony "virtues" I would be holding up and cramming down their throats, they would become mine! You see, if they hypnotically accepted my flowery words of truth, they would also be unconsciously accepting the malignant spirit behind those words. See how powerful evil is when draped in religious garb!

Love never pressures children toward anything. It is really your secret wickedness which causes you to apply pressure to your children, and that wicked nature is reflected in them, manifesting in either hypocrisy or bestiality—apparently opposite extremes. The classic parental panic syndrome does nothing but reinforce the particular problem that was first hatched by parental pressure. Your frustration literally feeds the wrong you have projected into your children, providing their resentful nature with the sweet nourishment of revenge. Anyone can derive this wicked kind of strength from someone else's struggle to reform him. Children can also feed on your guilt-based sympathy, taking advantage over and over again until you feel like disowning them or joining them for relief.

It is just possible that after struggling to change them, you may end up being changed *by* them. What else can you do but disown or accept your weird, wicked creations? Some parents actually chase after the perverts they have created all the way to hell. Their motive? To hold on to the false security of their love. Now it's the parents' turn to become the victims of a sub-culture lifestyle through their children's domination. They become super reverent and fearful of their children and of a vile system which is even lower than the social order which spawned them as parents.

Then comes the holocaust.

Baby egos come into the world inherently vulnerable to pressure and suggestible to sin. Without the protection of a loving parent, they are at the mercy of the world. For God's sake, don't *you* be a corrupting influence to them, too.

It is pain—the pain of sin at home in you—that compels you to make your children fail through pushing them to achieve. And they will be driven, just as you were, either to the failure of success or the outright failure of failure.

Under this system, which is born of pride, you are just as damned if you *don't* correct your children as if you do. You are helpless. You can only project the very evils you are trying to correct, because what lives in you also wants to live through your children; you prepare the way for it through emotionalizing them. The pain of your own dying to others forces you to try to recoup your energy loss through baiting your child. The hell in you survives through someone else's fall—such is the dog-eat-dog system under which we all live, making each other's lives wretched until the day we die. You are no better than the tyrant you hate, but the excruciating pleasure of your unearthly preoccupation with each other blocks you from seeing the harm you are doing.

Surely you have seen that children derive pleasure from teasing and inflicting pain on smaller kids. Street creeps get the same sort of pleasure and relief from pain by beating old ladies' heads in. Sad to say, most parents are on the same level; very few know the meaning of emotional maturity. They continue to enjoy that fiendish delight that comes through teasing and creating problems in their kids. (Children make especially good targets because they can't yet fight back.)

Many people can recall being degraded in some particular way as children, and then having the urge to do that same thing to someone else. The pain of your own personal suffering (at the hands of your cruel parents and others) drives you to seek the pleasure of having a victim of your very own. In your formative years, you were debilitated and drained of life through tease and challenge. When you become a parent, you find yourself seizing upon the opportunity to do the same thing. The moment a child is born, everyone begins systematically eating away at his guts.

Without realizing it, you pass on the nature you inherited to your own child while devouring his substance. Having fallen, you are part of a "food chain"—giving up life to your own personal tormentors, and trying to take it back by taking it out on your kids. It is such a relief to be cruel and impatient that you may not see the harm in it.

Why do you suppose classic horror movies can still rivet our attention? It is because they are a shocking reminder of *how things really are.* We are all like people bitten by vampires, a cast of zombies whose reward is to attain to vampire status ourselves. And never forget that somewhere behind the scenes there is an invisible daddy Dracula, feeding us lies and security, sucking in our life, drawing all humanity to himself.

Now take a second look at what it really means to take out your feelings of hostility on others. We are victims who serve and mimic our master. We may not want to hurt others, but are compelled to do so because of our own hurt.

A leader's special blood-sucking power and pseudo-happiness is proportionate to the mass of egos he can inspire (and degrade) through the appeal to their pride.

One can gain power through exhorting fools to dreams of power, glory and success. On the other hand, power can also be gained by degrading people. Indeed, there are many who are addicted to being punished and degraded; they feel loved and fulfilled through acts of cruelty. Either way, temptation is at work. The special effect of corruption, whether pleasant or unpleasant, is the bizarre feeling that one is becoming what the other person is. For many of us, that is the only way of ever becoming *anything.*

It is fairly common knowledge that a drug addict feels like a king attended by his pusher, when in reality the pusher is king. The victim rarely forsees his own destruction. He sees death as life, a movement forward toward greatness; to his psychotic ego, the process of physical dying is a very real survival need. And so it is with all sensual experience.

People die to their systems and to their cultures, and leaders feed on the masses like vampires and spiders, while Satan feeds and projects himself into us all.

For God's sake, save your children from a fate worse than death: change the polarity of your own soul from pride to humility. Only then will you experience the divine power coming through you, which has absolute authority over evil and errant behavior. You will have the strength and courage to sever your rebellious children from the hypnotic influence of their "friends." And for God's sake, throw those record players out of the house!

Children need authority; they can only grow in relationship to it. But false authority inflames a child's desire for forbidden things, especially those in which temptation comes disguised as goodness and light. "Don't" becomes "do." After that, any rescue attempt drives the victim deeper toward psychosis, mental aberrations, a life of sin, of crime or, perhaps, bizarre cult religions.

Fathers must realize that they have submitted themselves, through their own weakness, to the system under which women have been since the fall of man. And men must realize that, in order to save their children from sin, they themselves must be saved from their own private love/hate sexual addiction to "momma's" charms and aggravations. Remember the immutable rule concerning the feminine mystique: the comforter and the corrupter are one and the same spirit.

The corrupter is king!

The comforter is king!

One way or another, women are always trying to change men. But even the attempt to bring about "positive" change is really tantamount to temptation because, if the woman succeeded in her efforts, it would make her the creator of the man, *a role which rightfully belongs only to God.*

It is the man who ought to help the woman change and be saved from that which tempted the original pair in the Garden, through giving up his selfish use of her in favor of love. In this fashion, woman would be born of man, and man of God, as was the intended pattern. But man born of woman inherits a weakness which calls up reinforcement from his "creator"—putting her in the terrible dilemma of wondering what to do with her illegitimate offspring. She feels guilty for wanting to get rid of him, but to nurse and coddle him is an embarrassment too.

Irrational female behavior is directly proportionate to the age-old use which man calls love. Contrary to popular belief, less sex is better sex. Sex modified by an overriding concern for the woman's well-being produces the true fulfillment. When it is enjoyed this way, a man will want less sex so that he may experience the joy of true love that eventually transcends sex altogether.

Gentlemen, you will do well to realize that your sexual desires are the outcrop of the deep and mysterious original mortal failing of pride, which gives women unreasonable power. Then evil rules through her seductive influence, reducing male children to momma's boys, men to mice, drunks, homosexuals or violent beasts.

Full of pride and ambition, weak men cannot stand alone without the female ego-sexual support. Wrong men—ambitious men—need a mother or a wife to stand behind them; but who, may I ask, is standing behind her? The devil, of course.

In your apparent desire to do some imagined "good," you have unwittingly infected your offspring with some form of pride. Look carefully and you will see that part of the reason you did it was that your own ego was threatened by the selfhood and the relative innocence of your child. Your (inferior) ego is love and power-hungry. Your childhood traumas have made you the coward who becomes the bully to try to regain respect. Weak before the strong, you can't resist experiencing the relief which comes from being strong before the weak. As I said, we can relieve hurt by hurting others; it's the way of the dog-eat-dog world.

Pressure education contributes its share of destruction. Those who *do* rise ambitiously in the social order cling patriotically to the mother system, trampling all over their brothers to get the most rewarding spot, while those who rebel gravitate to their own reassuring, bloodsucking leaders. Thousands of drop-outs fall out of the system every year into the gutter, seeking success there.

You can see your kids being exploited by their fiend-friends. But what you can't see is that they can *see you* being taken in by *your* rotten system of friends and government. You can see what is wrong with others, but cannot see your own folly. The "progress" of pride carries with it the seeds of its own destruction.

Survival within any system to which you belong depends on your being treacherous, sly, ruthless, hypocritical and cruel. Leader-power depends on abandoning principles of honesty, motivating others through deceit and rewarding greed, selfishness, avarice, lust, thievery and exploitation. What a criminal chain gang of command we support in the name of country, religion and business!

No matter which way you slice it, we are all taken as we take. No one really minds though, because when we are taken, there arises in us a sense of duty to our selfish desires and to our leaders, and we find satanic delight as we carry out that "duty" through corrupting the innocent.

The street order differs from the accepted order of society only in that gutter people are more open about the vile and vicious things they do for kicks, power and glory. *All proud people feel they have the right to survive at any price, no matter who must pay it.* When they exercise this "right" to exist through someone else's suffering, it restores to them a temporary sense of dignity and power. Each kill feeds the implanted identity and makes it feel good. Hovering like a waiting vulture over souls who live by hook or by crook is yet another lying spirit, and over it, another. At the very end of the chain of human misery is some unseen, horrible thing sucking mankind unto himself. Believe it or not, parenthood is the threshold through which this inhuman system of things comes into existence.

Pain is the agony the soul feels as it dies and reawakens with Satan's nature. In our pride, we survive by manipulating and forcing others to give up their substance just the way we gave up ours. We have the devil's identity and we eat his soul food. Destruction is the devil's (re)creation. We have been dehumanized and recreated to serve a new master under a new system and we do his work, evangelize his way and receive his comforts.

This evil thing living within us all is constantly projecting itself and devouring succeeding generations. Children escape one brand of evil only to become trapped later in other ways. The Lord said that the sins (failures) of the fathers are visited (projected) unto the third and fourth generations of them that hate me.

Workers who have the simple skills to do their jobs and kids who have a natural eagerness to learn do not satisfy the lust of authorities, who need to be needed. So they pressure and tease, driven to destroy the natural order which would serve God and replace it with a system which they can administrate. In this world, death is great business.

The masses have always been debilitated and destroyed by cruel government, religion and heartless commerce. Parents come home drained by the pressures of inhuman work. Then what do they do? They take their frustrations out on their kids, laying waste their children's souls to drink from them the life to replace what they have lost to the system.

Now the violated child himself goes out seeking to retrieve life—beating up old ladies, getting kicks from drugs, music and booze.

If you do not find grace, you will be hurt, and hurt compels you to help yourself by passing on that hurt to others.

There are many subtle forms of temptation—for example, the old mother who scrubs floors so her son can go through medical school, hoping against hope that this supreme sacrifice will gain her son's respect. Like this old woman, many martyrs have a secret selfish goal for which they are sacrificing themselves; thus they end up being taken. You know the unhappy ending. As a rich doctor, the son's big, fat, spoiled ego feels too superior to associate with his grasping, sniveling (and yes—manipulating, glory-seeking) mother. He might even throw her into the poorhouse to live out her wretched life alone with the rejection and resentment she has been set up to enjoy. Without realizing it, mother created a cruel and evil monster; the prideful nature she encouraged in her son in hopes that it would adore her, turned instead on its creator.

By hook or by crook does the tempter kill—the effect is always the same. Whether he stands in the pulpit, exciting and glorifying hypocritical sheep, or rules as a rabble-rousing Hitler, extolling the virtues of evil, his power is gained from turning on his followers; these, in turn, fill *their* egos from those underlings whom they can find to destroy. Surely this must explain such inhuman phenomena as Nazi Germany and the mayhem perpetrated throughout the ages at the hands of religious maniacs. Religious conscripts are obliged to degrade others to soothe the pain of their own surrender. They accomplish this through the cruelty of forcing religion down their children's throats and by torturing the people around them—applying enormous, unbearable pressure—in the name of saving their souls. Child abuse by such psychic methods is commonplace.

We are all effects of a cause, seeking to be causes ourselves. We are events seeking the power to make things happen. Desperately we strive to imprint, impress and affect others in order to know ourselves as gods—and, God, what destructive effects we have! We actually get satisfaction from destroying the things around us; we work like hell to break others down to build ourselves up. Whether we realize it or not, *we always revitalize ourselves at other people's expense.*

Whoever reacts to guile, whether they are tortured or seduced, gives up life-force and power, *and that power is temporary relief to the tormentor.* Then the tormentor, in turn, is tormented and drained by one still higher in the dog-eat-dog chain gang.

Untold violence is done in the name of molding good citizens, provoking more violence in response to the injustices of hypocrisy. Noble reasons may be given to justify the process, but what it amounts to is creating a vehicle, powered by weakness of the people, in which the fat cats in the political and criminal world ride to success.

Two forces are at work here, both emanating from the same source. Satan tempts you to break the law on the one hand so he can enslave you by enforcing the law on the other. Now see the dilemma your children are in. Everyone who wants to help them really wants to help himself *to* them. Everyone wants a little piece of the action. Even when the victims do see how they have been deceived, their pride, which has grown more guilty, tends to make them reach outward for reassurance again, sinking even lower, away from the shaming but redeeming light.

You are the one who ought to protect your child from the abyss of evil, but you cannot if you are still part of the system of pride. Your "help" will hurt, because you represent the wrong type of authority, just as your parents, fools that they were, represented to you.

Nevertheless, when all is said and done, have compassion on your poor old mom and dad. Mother never knew a proper father or husband to love her and correct her. How could she touch you with the correcting love she had never known? Your father's mother set his ego up to enjoy your mother's wrong and to cultivate it to support the wrong in him. So her ugliness grew with the power dad gave her to destroy you. Bear this in mind—your parents may have wanted to do right by you in part, but the spoiled, ignorant part of them was stronger and had its way, tempting you and feeding on your confusion.

Resist the temptation to hate your parents' injustice and you will begin to discover how to stop drawing up violence in your own children. *Innocence is your only protection!* Evil cannot draw substance from or project its nature into those who have found salvation. Yearn for faith and patience, which will form a shield, a perfect force field that will protect both you and your family from the biting chills of hell. Through patience, which cannot hurt or be hurt, comes the correcting force of love.

3: Weak Fathers, Fierce Mothers: The Reasons

Fierce wives are the by-products of docile husbands. Fierce and drinking wives are by-products of men who seek to appease their wives' displeasure through the classic ways of buying affection and giving in to displays of anger—as if that would make them good guys.

Abdicating their roles as husbands and fathers, such men tempt their wives to take on the manly role of disciplinarian, thereby tempting the children to rebel. Picking up the gauntlet of challenge, the female rises to the occasion (often pridefully and resentfully) only to fall flat on her face because she lacks the natural authority which would command the children's respect. Left alone with her brood of Frankensteins, she finds she must either indulge them or resort to violence to maintain a semblance of order in the home.

Whether she wants to or not, the average female tends to weaken and dominate her man. Once she gets into the driver's seat, she becomes a miserable, irritating witch. No matter how hard she has struggled to get there, she is inevitably unhappy behind the wheel because she knows deep down that she is an unsafe driver. Her female identity melts away through a confusing haze of impatience and contempt and she becomes tainted with masculinity. Then the part-male, part-female, part-devil identity in her cries out to the man in her life for correcting love, only to be answered by him with sex and failing.

What, then, does a wife really need? Her soul cries out to be subdued, purged and changed by the power of true love. All this is not surprising, because any uncorrected creature worthy of the name woman will resent a weak husband. Nearly all her frustrations are caused by men giving in and giving power to her guileful teasing and to her rage.

The responsibility of rearing the young does not ultimately belong to the woman. Just as the choice to bring children into the world rests with the man, so is the moral responsibility for their welfare given into his hands. Because woman was not created to play the male role, children automatically attempt to rebel against accepting her authority. *For any child to accept the impatient, seductive authority of a female is to surrender his soul to evil.*

Many women are unaware of how their bodies are employed by evil to undermine male authority, to trick the sons of man into rejecting the spirit of the father and accepting the sick, guileful spirit operating through momma! The ultimate duty of a father is to correct the inherited, prideful nature in the mother; he must save the children from the woman, and the woman from herself.

A variation of this Adam and Eve syndrome occurs in so-called "reform" or "correctional" institutions. Correction, when it comes from womanish authorities (those who, like seductive females, gain positions of power through stealth and craft), only hardens the criminals, thus justifying the need for an ever-increasing army of momma-reformers, all of whom enjoy playing God at the inmates' expense. Like the fierce "mommas" they really are, those reformers have nothing but contempt for the weak, submissive "husband" inmates. At the same time, they are driven to punish the rebels mercilessly, always driving them to greater violence. For all their so-called reforming, reformers are a miserable, guilty lot. Indeed, they become worse than those they are trying to save. It is none other than the ancient, guileful serpent operating in them (again offering what he cannot deliver), who is raising up the promise of reform and following through with a hellish spirit which only knows how to coddle or to punish people. It spoils them rotten, then punishes them for *being* rotten.

We are born into an environment of sexual politics where such reformers rule the roost. Like the sheep they are, people who are without Godly grace or manly guts can't find it in themselves to put these "big momma" politicians and bureaucrats in their places; they react helplessly in the age-old styles of rebellion or of mindless conformity. Society demonstrates in a political macrocosm the principle of the weak husband giving power to the wife. A class of part-men, part-women, part-devils has evolved which thrives on the effects of teasing the populace. And, spineless weaklings that we are, we (the husband people) *deserve* to suffer at the hands of those ravening wolves.

Inherited pride will always cause institutions and wives to go mad with power eventually. Men, feeling trapped and emasculated, hoping to compensate for the loss of spiritual power, often resort to violence and end up in revolt, beating their wives into the ground—if they are able to, that is. Similarly, the masses, when they are unable to take any more suffering, occasionally rise up with terrible violence and topple the giants from their thrones of power, only to become just like the very thing they hated once they take over. Nothing changes. In fact, as the wheel turns, things get worse.

The breakdown of family life begins with the default of the father's authority. Spoiled and rebellious, the children wander out into the world soliciting reinforcement for their troubled identities. Sex, politics, religion, the occult, medicine, music, education and drugs are just some of the endless varieties of temptation that are lurking in the shadows, waiting to claim them.

The losing husband often manages to get some kicks by dumping his responsibility on the dominant woman, while he stands by, watching her struggle and fail with the children. There he sits like a mocking bird on a perch, safe from criticism, judging himself into self-righteous ecstasy. In his corrupt, perverted, scheming, unprincipled soul, he is no longer the object of wifely derision— he has distorted failure into triumph. That is exactly what all losers do when they have no hope of winning; they simply place the winners on pedestals and "let" them run everything, knowing full well that they are sure to make a bloody mess of everything in the end.

The violent father, on the other hand, is the product of a too-submissive (battle-fearful) wife. Giving in to a man and keeping him "happy," free from anger and criticism, happens to be the secret way many females conquer their mates. When the male begins to suspect that he has been had, he tries to compensate for the loss of real authority with animal force. For a time, a woman can keep a man from being angry by pacifying him with sex but, sooner or later, that man will catch on and learn to use violence as a means of obtaining sex-love.

The stage is set for a vicious cycle to occur. The nicer the frightened woman is to the man (hoping to placate his rage) the more violent he becomes. If she is backed against the wall enough, she may become violent as a last resort, which only justifies his judgment upon her.

I know a woman who, before her enlightenment, was so distressed over her husband's impatience and subtle cruelties toward their son that she tried to drain off her husband's excessive tensions and hostilities toward the boy by pacifying the husband with more sex and greater subservience. She didn't realize (until the damage was done) that she was making a fiend out of her husband, a whore out of herself and driving her son into homosexuality and an eventual deep psychosis. A sick son and a broken home became her reward for trying to manipulate the situation by using sensual methods. Fortunately, she knows now that weakness becomes wickedness. She knows not to play the Eve game any more.

In situations like this, it may be hard for a woman to see what power she really has, because she appears to be the one being dominated, enslaved, and used. She can go on for years thinking she is the sole victim. Believing herself to be innocent, however, prevents her from seeing her real role as Dr. Frankenstein, stalked and terrified by the monster she herself has made.

It is a heavy responsibility for a woman to face up to what has really been happening, and when finally she begins to see it, she may not think herself ready. Hating, blaming and fearing the monster, she continues to provide the kind of excitement which made the monster what it is. "Love" (agreement) shapes the monster, but rejection also serves to fire its nature.

A female can't win if she doesn't have the right kind of husband. She is damned if she rejects him and damned if she agrees with him. When a woman marries out of vanity, it is like choosing death over life.

Guile is what makes a woman appear exciting and attractive to begin with, and guile is what a man must learn to correct if he is to survive. Conquer he must, if a man is to survive the terrible power of a female's "love."

It is true that a female must be exciting if she wants a man, but while a man can enjoy those charms for a season, he must eventually come to spiritual terms with a woman's ensnaring love. He ought to become the source of true love and comfort, thereby releasing her from the compulsion to attend to his unwholesome needs.

Since the beginning of man's time on earth, family troubles have revolved around the woman, *but the fault has always been with the way man uses her charm to support his ego.* To *use* is to fail with everything. Were it not for man's ego-weakness for use, evil would not survive long in this world.

The entire morbid history of mankind is based on the interaction of weak men and crafty women. From the tyranny of homes to the tyrannies of nations, the Adam-and-Eve syndrome is the principle behind all despotism and destruction. It is the dope addict's ego-need which brings into being and draws to him the evil pusher, literally changing ordinary men into slave traders. The addict's need draws hell into existence to serve his pride.

43

When an adversary intrigue does not already exist, people will go out and *create* the torture scenes they need, like bored kids playing cops and robbers. *A sinner is afraid of true freedom.* He needs the security of the slavish psychotic state, and there is always a resident psychopath ready to oblige.

Need and the need-to-be-needed is a slave-tyrant game as old as that of beauty and the beast. One moment the beast is exploited by the beauty and the next the beauty is battered around by the beast. Women live in terror of the beast of their own creation.

"Protecting" the children from their violent father is often a wife's devious means of jockeying for the power position. Indeed, the classic way of destroying a man's authority is to drive him to violence through alternately teasing him with sex and nagging him with petty cruelties. The children then tend to reject the father's wickedness and accept the mother's "goodness." If the mother were truly interested in protecting her children, she would start being honest with her husband, but guile strikes her dumb. She cannot speak the truth without losing the feeling of power and security which his weakness excites in her; without the security of true love which comes from within, she has nothing else. And for that feeling of power, she teases the life out of everyone around her.

As long as we have any ambitions, goals or will to succeed, we cannot speak the truth, because truth offends those with whom we wish to succeed. One simply cannot have one's own selfish way when one is completely honest, and that is why women are not straightforward with men. Sooner or later, though, they must pay a heavy price for such dishonesty.

Pride prohibits a man from loving an honest woman because he cannot lose himself in her sexually. It is difficult for a woman to get a man unless she represents herself as a use/sex object. It is through playing this game of "love" that women receive terrible power.

Ladies, can you see how important it is for you to be modest? Men have enough problems with lust without your making it worse, so refrain from being sexually aggressive. The effect of tempting a man into sexual activity is to create in him a *dependence* upon being tempted, robbing him of his own natural aggression. The guilt of functioning out of season can make him degenerate further and begin to demand strange and bizarre sexual rituals. That can threaten your "security" and make you feel like a whore, or it may cause you to tease him about not being enough of a man for you—and you know the rest of the story!

Just as the male animal becomes addicted to tease, females also become addicted to being teasers. Once addicted to sapping the male life-essence which comes through his failing love (sex), the whorish, frustrated, desperate and vindictive female monster goes on to destroy the rest of her family.

As I mentioned before, female tease represents "life," and men thrive on making their women mad to bring out of them the two kinds of tease they need (anger and sex). A man likes a witchy, sexy wife because she reminds him of his mother (whom his father loved).

Surely you have heard the old cliché, "Darling, you look beautiful when you are angry." Men thrive on tease. Teasers look beautiful to those in need; anyone who has the power to hold attention away from the awful reality of what one has become looks beautiful and special. Anyone who makes us feel good or special *is* special to us, and we love to get lost in the lie of it all.

Look at it from another point of view: the tease for power is also a cry for correction. *A woman's imperfection teases because it needs correction,* just as a child's imperfections tease for parental love. If a parent gives in to and appeases the nag, that parent is feeding the monster in that child. As a result, the naughty child becomes worse and desperately cries out again for love. Weaker now, the parent gives in more easily and the vicious cycle is perpetuated. I tell you truly, in your failing you will suffer by seeing the destruction of your own family.

When she does not know the security of true love, a woman derives her satisfaction by being the lover herself. But when she takes this role, she is compelled, like the black widow spider, to destroy her beloved in the process.

It is good to pause here and remember the dispassionate rule for dealing with all of this properly: remain distant and neutral toward whatever is happening. It will save your soul.

Remember the lesson: have compassion and resolve your resentment toward your parents; cease projecting the parent you needed and hated into your lover. If you can become aware enough to do that, you will no longer infect your children as your parents did you. Bear in mind that we are dealing with sin passed from generation to generation through the weakness of pride.

When you feel trapped in your role as a man-woman or woman-man, be careful how you try to get free. It is useless to struggle. You must observe your dilemma calmly and own up to your part in creating it. You must not give way to that something within which fears the truth and thrives on resentment.

It was your inability to be objective that got you into trouble in the first place. You were born into an accursed atmosphere and you immediately began taking shape through the tease of injustice, *because you reacted to it with resentment.*

Mother's identity possesses and drives you. Men seek it out in women; women are fascinated with other women and with their mother's identity in men. It is common for mother-dominated women to seek out and punish that female identity in their husbands. They attempt to overcome their fear of being dominated by finding someone to dominate. (That is what makes those nice, weak, obliging men appealing and exciting to you. The sweet, gentle, submissive fellow you thought was a good man is really a woman inside.)

Mother has planted something of her image and spirit in your mind, which seeks and projects the mother-nature in others. Mother is even inside your head, mentally driving you and feeding on your energies just as she always has in person. You are mistaken if you think you hate your father—it is all a clever distraction. Mother simply set dad up as an object of rejection in order to trick you into accepting her as God. Underneath any enslaving, binding love you might feel for her has got to be resentment.

The implanted identity in you uses the mother-love/hate-tease to sustain itself, a man in his way and a woman in her way. That same sick spirit within teaches you how to set up objects of love and hate, just as it taught your parents how to use each other (and you).

47

There is tease on two fronts; the intrigue outside distracts you from seeing the evil operating within yourself, which is meanwhile taking its toll on your kids.

The sick mind cannot tolerate emotional freedom because *therein is truth*. That is why we are all so involved in sustaining ourselves and losing ourselves through emotional intrigue.

One person always portrays the tyrant, the other, the slave. The intrigue of loving and being loved, or hating and being hated, provides pleasure through distraction for both. We find pleasure in hurting and in being hurt, because the pleasure of "making up" (sex) is intensified after a fight. Since hating makes sexing more pleasurable, the syndrome is bound to create a living hell for your children. Born in sin, they are formed in your unchastened image and likeness which projects from generation to generation. Now your own spiritual refinement depends on dealing with your children properly

But hold on! I am not writing this so that you can have a reason to blame your parents. They, as people, did not cause your suffering; they were merely instruments, ignorant bodies through which your private hell came into being. By all means, hate evil; but you can't hate evil by hating your parents. To hate each other is to embrace and agree with evil; that is exactly how the evil gets to possess you!

God's law requires that we love one another in a special way. Resentment merely serves the purpose of the teaser; it blocks true love and makes you a slave of the spirit behind the tease. Love (patience, forgiveness and long-suffering) will release you from the spirit of your mother. It may even release mother from herself. Love comes by simply understanding that others are prisoners, just as you are. Understanding brings compassion.

True love is not so much what you get, but what you give (up). Therefore, pass up the sweet meat of resentment (judgment) and defeat the purpose of hell. Look at how you are with your children and see the truth— which is that you can no more stop yourself from hurting them than your parents could stop hurting you. From deeply realizing this, true compassion will develop toward your parents and an unselfish love for your children and your spouse.

It is folly for a man to seek a spiritual woman; rather, he should look for one who *recognizes* his authority, sincerity and strength, and who is willing to take correction and follow his leadership. We are speaking now of a man who is worthy of such respect and obedience, which is not the same thing as a man put on a pedestal by a woman. A guileful woman will often worship a man (no matter what he's really like) as a means of conquering him. Let me illustrate this with the example of a man whose witchy mother drove her husband to suicide. The way the son dealt with the spirit of his mother within him was to marry a "sweet" woman who appeared to be just the opposite. I am afraid this man will go to his grave never understanding the purpose for which he was created, because he is so involved with this super-sweet, understanding creature. He has cultivated in her the perfect mother into whom he escapes from his imperfect mother. His wife's security rests on not giving him a hard time; therefore, he can never muster the strength and love to conquer, to fight the good fight for her sake. He can never really oppose the false sweetness in the woman's nature. He can't save himself from her, or the woman from herself, because he is too busy sustaining himself with her. *The saving love and respect that a woman needs to experience with a man can only grow from his being tested and not found wanting.* When a woman can have such belief in a man, it can save her from herself.

Men who are not believable must try to escape the wicked-witch identity sown in them by their mothers through identifying with someone else's beautiful-witch identity. They run from one woman to another for this effect, only to eventually discover the horror lurking behind the beauty. Indeed, the entire doctrine of psychopolitics rests on this same principle of giving the people new "beautiful people" to love them and never letting the masses awaken to the truth of their "only-a-mother-could-love-it" ugliness. "Beautiful people" are like opiates, keeping the masses from opposing authority by never letting them awaken.

Similarly, the "perfect" woman who perfectly pleases her man, who keeps him from the pain and suffering of seeing his own failing, *will surely kill him* by letting him think all is well so that he never seeks God's salvation. Many women are attracted to such ignorant donkeys. The female ego-fear of being dominated and the desire to rule evolve the seductive craft of keeping male egos gloriously asleep, while the victims (who don't see they are victims) lap it up!

Of all temptations, the most dangerous is "perfection." The kind of phony perfection which is all-loving, all-forgiving, always supportive, comforting, sympathetic and agreeable, is from the netherworld, and such will drain away your life. How can one oppose or deal with evil when it is so entertaining, when it retreats behind a sexy body or the Bible, presenting a facade of Christian love?

A good marriage is a good fight. With life in general, there is a good fight and there is a bad fight. The bad fight is to struggle out of rage and fear. But *never* to fight is also bad.

People often throw the baby out with the bath water. They remember how their parents fought like cats and dogs and they blame *marriage* because of what it did to them. How wonderful it would have been to have seen a father stand up and fight for the woman's life against the unreasonable spirit that possessed her! No man can do this marvelous thing as long as his ego needs what is wrong with the woman, to tease and give life to what is wrong with him. If and when the prideful male does fight, it is only out of rage, to rise above his enslavement. To reject the sanctity of marriage simply because your parents failed is a serious error. As in a democracy, marriage requires great integrity in order to succeed. It is not marriage, nor is it democracy, which falls short; it is *people* who fail those systems.

Naziism cannot work for good because it is a sick system which requires sick people, but democracy and marriage can work because they are sound in principle. It is human nature which fails these systems. The systems end up getting the blame and getting thrown out. What is left is demoralization and dehumanization, which lead inexorably to moral decay and then to dictatorship.

As a concession to man's fallen nature, and to fulfill His purposes, God sanctified marriage. Marriage is the *only* framework in which sex can be permitted. Here it can be

51

practiced with awareness and understanding.

As we descend from perfection, the procreative impulse appears as the mortal outgrowth of *original* sin. Sex itself is not (necessarily) a sin, but pride in it is. That is why one must never take pride in sex. To take pride in *anything* is to lose oneself in the fault one should be observing, learning from and rising above.

To take pride in sex is to reject the truth concerning what it means in terms of original failing. Repeating the original sin is what intensifies sensual impulses. Ambitious, proud men are always sex addicts, something like drug addicts. Sex becomes a death-fixation.

While most other addictions can be immediately resolved and transcended through understanding and repentance, sex can only be modified and upgraded. Sex communication is the basis of our earth-bound, mortal existence; the ego's sensuous nature would cease to exist without it. A very special dispensation from God is required to lift us beyond sex love. Until then, practice sex with love. Begin, gentlemen, by giving up resentment when you are rejected. Be patient and understanding. Don't promote a woman to need you or to accept you.

Marriage was never meant to be a picnic. It is a *framework* wherein man can express his weakness and work out his ancient problem. Marriage is where both husband and wife suffer from their failures to understand its mystery in a way that makes them cry out to God for His answer.

At a certain point in marriage, even when sex has been practiced with love, sexual episodes are followed by anxiety, by feelings of regret, and by a mysterious feeling that one has failed and must "start all over again."

Everything in us may tell us that sex is the way to eternal life, and yet something else says it is not. "Take from her something, give to her something, and live forever" is Dracula's creed.

We who are loyal to God's rules of marriage are conscious of the weakening and aging effect of sex. One can be aware of its destructive effects outside of marriage too, but here the sin makes people reject the truth about what they are doing, making them want to lose themselves more and more in lust. Outside marriage, there can be nothing but vain use and the vain use of the user. The guilt of it enmeshes the user ever more deeply in his need for the used.

This is not to say that marriage is necessarily holy. Marriage *can* be pure, while living together cannot. "Swinging" is a lifestyle in which honor, sincerity and commitment can play no part, and the guilt from the experience causes the soul to fear and reject the truth continually. This truth happens to be the understanding which could raise the soul and the nature beyond mortality, unto eternal life; that is what we deny ourselves when we are moved by unbridled desire.

In summary, let me illustrate the principle of trauma and show you how it can trace the course of sex love back to original sin. Suppose I pushed you into the water and you couldn't swim. Chances are that you would grow up to be either fascinated with water or afraid of it. In your ongoing struggle with the way the water affected you, I could be forgotten as the perpetrator of your trauma. You could literally burn yourself out compensating for the fear of water by becoming the world's greatest swimmer, or you might simply waste away, consumed by a growing terror. *Water* would appear to be the problem against which you must struggle and the cause of the problem would always remain hidden. The wicked spirit which pushed you in would still be pushing you secretly. Triumphant, it would still be the moving force egging you on to struggle your life away. Evil doesn't much care whether you "succeed" as the world's greatest swimmer or fail, because you will have given up your life either way.

Transfer this principle to your sex problems. Are you now the world's greatest lover, seeking conquest after conquest over the female mystique, or are you afraid of sex, needing the woman and yet fearing the encounter? Why are you so preoccupied with sex? *So you can not grow to be what you should be.* The spirit which caused your problem with sex is always around teasing you with it.

To give you another example—in drug addiction, drugs are not the problem but the spirit of the pusher is. Of course, the underlying cause of the problem is the addict's ego-need for reassurance. It is the sinner's *use* that enslaves him. A person would have no problem at all were it not for his pride. In his willful struggle to be free from drugs, booze or cigarettes (or in his continued abuse of them), the victim forgets the real problem, which is his *weakness.* Such ego-struggle only creates a greater need for reassurance, because struggle itself is another failing.

The female form conceals and embodies the original tease, and man's prideful struggle for or against the woman always involves him more deeply with fighting or sexing, never allowing him to discover what love is. Sexing leads to fighting and fighting leads to sexing, until man and woman finish each other off, never having been free for one single moment to ponder the meaning of life.

4: The Meddling Mother

Although you may want the best for your child, the way you speak, the tone of your voice, the timing, all act to prevent it. Become too strong and you could have rebellion on your hands, or a child who is only good because he is afraid to be bad. Watch out when you are not around! A "liberator" will come like a knight in shining armor, a really bad person who will "free" him from the sterile tyranny of your holier-than-thou straightjacket of restraint.

Sure, you speak the truth. Perhaps you really want to set your child straight; you point out when and where he is wrong. But the reason it backfires in your face is that you lack force. You are too weak; you are not a proper example. You have no authority, or you are the wrong kind of authority.

Perhaps you fear using force because in the past it did more harm than good. So you speak up tenderly, trying to do good *without offending or upsetting anyone*. You may fear to be a (parental) force for good because what you experienced in the past, at the hands of your own parents, was cruel and based on anger. As a parent, you know what it is like to be hated. You know what children feel and think. What you don't know is that, under the ego system of hate and love, we create the very thing we fear most by taking an opposite position. With your kind of "love" you may well raise up your parents' nature in your offspring.

A child's pride is tempted to take advantage and to swell up in response to anger or to a weak show of love. By being honest but ineffective, weak and hypocritical, you excite and feed a child's larceny. In turn, your child can cultivate your weakness and make you think that you are a kind mother, in order to take advantage of you. Believe me, you could work yourself to death for nothing.

The force behind true love enables you to endure the feedback of hateful persecutions you might have to bear. Back-biting, name-calling, persecution and rejection are all part and parcel of your own growing up. You can handle that because, deep down, love knows such suffering without the attendant resentment which drives one to surrender with the weakness of false love. Your steadfastness may well be your persecutor's only chance for deliverance.

Humanistically speaking, those warm puppy-love feelings we like to generate and feel for one another are a counterfeit love. Because we *feel* good for making another feel divine, we think that *is* good. If you will only look carefully, you will notice that this "feeling good for making others feel good" is a selfish trick.

We have all misunderstood what great men of the past have had to say about love; we have misinterpreted the law or the word that exhorts us to loving kindness. We have tried to fit God's concept of love into *our own* egotistical way of thinking. We have become sympathetic and supportive as an excuse for seeking support for our selfish pride. We love gently, not to offend egos, in order to be adored in return. Our consideration is never for others, but to please ourselves. Have I not explained the kind of "love" that teases and tempts a soul to tumble? Don't thieves and robbers love thieves and robbers? Must not your love be different from theirs?

Surely you don't want to support someone in his weakness. Isn't that the kind of thing you would expect from a whore or a devil, a liar and a cheat, someone who puts you on to cheat you out of your money or your life?

We are ignorant of the fact that truly great men like Jesus loved with *a special kind of non-worldly love,* the kind which had the courage to rebuke, shame and offend the pride of men so that they might change. The love of these great men certainly did *not* conform to a thief-loving-thief, love-you-as-you-are formula.

Therefore, a certain kind of "offense" is the key to salvation—yours and theirs.

Direct, unemotional honesty has a cutting edge and offers an opportunity for your child to make a meaningful change. Be direct so as to break through defenses with a forceless shock, that is, force without the usual (resentment-backed) pressure so as to literally throw them back on themselves. They will end up looking at what *they* are doing wrong, rather than at what you are doing wrong or the way you are going about doing "right."

If you have the calm innocence to tell it like it is without anger or fear, then you become a catalyst for meaningful change rather than a stimulus to phony surface behavior.

When you are patient, you never feel that sense of failure or triumph. You don't feel responsible for the outcome, only for what you must say or do. Rest assured that firm outspokenness reaches in, deep down, all the way through the marrow to the roots of the soul itself, in a way that helps, not hurts. That is, it helps with a good hurt, not hurts with a "help," the way worldly love does.

But look what happens when your ego, in its spiritual poverty, with its own need for love and with its fear of offending, speaks up about this or that issue. Because of need, you dare not go as far as you must. You cannot effectively change or offend egos from whom you need support. So your prideful "truth," lacking real force for good, literally ends up giving a transfusion of strength to the wrong. As long as there is pride in whatever you do, you cannot save *others* from pride. You challenge it, you cater to it, and you make that ugly thing in them grow to feed the ugly thing in you.

Some children resent your ineffectiveness so much that they find themselves rebelling against the good things you want for them, even though they also want them for themselves deep down in their hearts. Most children are contemptuous: they feel resentment toward parents for not being strong and loving enough to save them from themselves, even going so far as to punish parents for failing them. Yes, you told them all right, but deep down they know (even if you don't), because they are on the receiving end, that the reason you are not effective is that *you don't really care for them at all.* What you care *more* about is what they think of you. That is what comes across to them. They sense you are carefully cultivating sickness in them to serve a sick need you have for them.

They hate your craven need passing itself off as love. Their hate produces such great torment inside them that it could make them end up bowing to your wishes to relieve that pain—but that doesn't work either; it makes the agony worse. When you find that your phony kindness appears to work, you might be so overjoyed that you reward them with more of the same phony love, which drives them clean up the wall—to suicide perhaps; to acts of violence, even against you. Why do they want to hurt you? Because they want to stop you from hurting them through your "loving" them.

The sick and guilty ego needs sustaining love. The hopes and glories of pride involve the admiration game. Instinctively your prideful nature knows it cannot expose others to themselves and still expect to get the support and "respect" it needs. You also sense that once corrected, a person can *never* serve you (or anyone) again. The game of pride would be over, and pride, fearing the Hell of ceasing to exist, is threatened. Were your children to find true innocence again, your ego's pain would be unbearable. You see, no ego in its wrong mind can do away with the evils it needs for support. It cannot speak up, and if it does, it cannot do so in a way that brings the good out of another.

The power to be effective cannot exist within the framework of the pride-ego system, but even if it did, you would never employ this power (of love) to destroy the ground of your own being. All that is left is words: ineffective, ego-soothing, manipulating, tender, hypocritical, meaningless words. Later come emotional, angry words, words which do more harm than good, even if they are technically correct. Words spoken in a moment of weakness and tenderness, or words of Truth spoken in rage, cause people to reject the very values that could otherwise save them. Pride, in cultivating evil to serve it, often ends up doing the serving. And that, my friend, is a taste of hell on earth.

If a man cannot fire his employee, it's usually because he has been too close to him. As a guilty boss, he has a need to be caught up (away from his guilt) through being popular. You may realize a supporting friend, husband or wife is entirely out of order, but if you either remain silent or speak to them about their fault ever so gently, in a patronizing way, you are assured the continued support you need.

Through being nice about this or that, you hope to *seduce* your friends from taking liberties while you hold fast to their respect for your ego. Dale Carnegie taught this heresy in his book, "How to Win Friends and Influence People." People may love your tact and warmth, the way you indulge their faults; and they may be very obliging, bowing worshipfully (but superficially) to your "greatness." Although you may develop a positive style of having your own way, winning friends and influencing people, you can never do good or bring anyone to the Truth. Outclassed by your devilish charm, people set you up as a teacher, a successful example after which to pattern their own rotten, selfish lives. In that sense only—and with those kinds of people—will you be a success.

In all meaningful relationships, there must be a crackle of *fire*, a special sparkle in the atmosphere which alone can bring about *meaningful change* without being the source of that change. Wherever you have people who are too considerate, comforting, friendly, obliging and inoffensive, you could end up in a sterile world wherein both parties become regressively weaker and more wicked, programmed to act politely and thoughtfully, but addicted to the process. Underneath the charade there is a secret but familiar frustration and rage, for although we may enjoy being comfortable, we sense our baby-wickedness is growing, being cultivated to serve a greater evil. Sure, we are loved, but only for the usefulness of our weakness or our wickedness.

Sooner or later we all get trapped into friendliness by one of those "wonderful," super-syrupy, bubbly persons. One day the mask falls away to reveal the demon lurking behind. Enraged now, we can't change our conduct or speak up without resentment. The spirit of anger speaks, and after that comes remorse and the spirit of phony love.

Resentment gives rise to guilt. It makes you feel as though you wronged this demon, and guilt forces your pride to make the demon a god, to seek from it a "redeeming love."

The world abounds in demons in human form, seeking to "save" angry, resentful, guilty souls with their phony love. Knowing this, why do you go on loving your child in this way?

Few children understand what they need. Feed their egos with phony love and they could grow to be slaves of "love"; secretly hating your love and your betrayal of them, their resentment eventually drives them to seek another lover and betrayer.

Observing their weakness for you, their addiction, you may come to believe that you are the greatest. But sure as hell, tragedy lies ahead. You can make your children into cripples with no direction of their own, looking to "the great You" for more and more guidance and support. One day you could find yourself enslaved to these helpless masses of protoplasm, who are slyly manipulating you through the very sickness you gave them. Nervous breakdown, anyone?

Coming down from your heaven to fill a need you yourself have created can take more and more out of what you ("god") cannot replace. Soon they are doing less and less for themselves and you are doing more and more for them. What a shock it is for "god" to discover that he is the slave of his own good-for-nothing, wretched creations. Deep resentment can send you straight to the funny farm or to the nearest bar.

Every love (need) people appear to have evolves out of the pain of pride's failing, enhanced by a terrible rage and resentment. People are often afraid of showing that resentment for fear of losing the love they need, even though the love they get upsets them more. Besides, many enjoy their secret judgments. They can use you when you "love" them, only to enjoy you again later as an object of (secret) contempt.

So, as much as your love "helps," that much more does it hurt. Their helplessness cries out to you for help; your guilt drives you again and again to lose yourself in the ego-gratification of "helping" them and making them worse.

All problems evolve from a worldly, prideful love and hate. You hate because you don't get enough love; then when you do get it, you hate it because it is the wrong kind! Your children are in trouble because you give them this terrible love and wonderful hate as a heritage.

*   *   *   *   *

Having become responsible for your child's downfall, you are inevitably faced with the problem of engineering his salvation. That is where you magnify both of your problems and come unglued. You have to get out of your child if you want to save him.

The problem is that you have become your child's god; which is to say that every time he suffers, his cry calls you down from heaven to answer his need. You simply must learn to resist answering his need like God from Heaven, getting in the way of his own internal, *real,* spiritual answer. *You* are the cause of the problem and the only answer your child has ever known. Now, because you are the cause and also the wrong answer, he suffers from the conflict your meddling sows in him.

You have to learn how to be concerned rather than worried. In concern there is genuine love, but in worry there is phony concern. Your ego can revel in worry because worry is an activity of the mind that can help you forget your failing and seem noble. Worry helps you to escape into thinking, from knowing what you are really like. A problem (child) challenges you to forget your failure but appeals to you, "god," to produce an answer. Saving your child is a way your ego grows and evolves away from Reality in an attempt to become that Reality, neatly spoiling your child in the process of saving yourself—saving face, really. It's hard to resist the cries of your beloved. Not knowing any other god greater than yourself, you are (un)naturally compelled to respond to need with the ecstasy of judgment or sympathy. Judgment hurts you both so much that it compels you to give sympathy, and sympathy becomes as much a problem as resentment was (and still is). Resentment puts your spirit in him, and sympathy sustains the exchange; or sympathy puts your spirit in him, and resentment sustains that exchange—either way.

That self in him now cries out in need to you who put it there, and you cannot resist comforting your self in him. It is always *your* spirit in your child that needs you and hates you for his own need for you. That is the basis of his conflict and yours.

Now perhaps you understand what I mean when I say you must get out of your child: back off, butt out of his life!

Will you resist the temptation to worry so that you might learn the meaning of true concern? Can you resist the temptation to minister unto his needs like a meddling god? Do you now see how you hurt with your help? Do you have the humility to realize that you *cannot* help? If you really want to help—don't!

Certainly you will feel pain not responding to his cry, but it is only the pain of your past guilt catching up with you, which you have lost sight of by losing yourself in your beloved's problems.

Mother's love, without the balance of a father's love, is part of the problem; mother's hate is the other part. Mother, you are the cause of your child's suffering, and you are making him worse by helping him. Seeing this Truth is the beginning of the miracle you both need. Woman, you have destroyed your husband with your love, and now you are destroying your children. Your own wicked need for love drives you to give love to get love. You must see what this need for love is: a misguided need to be god.

Do you really want to help? Then resist the temptation to respond to need with "love" or hate (resentment).

64

True concern comes as you abandon the pleasures of worry. There is no need to teach about loving concern; it is there, buried underneath all that worry.

I am not saying "don't worry," which can mean, "Don't worry, think of something else, wash your hands of the whole mess!" No, I am not saying "don't care," but I am saying back off! Become objective to the activity of your own mind, into which you are escaping from failing and guilt by being involved with a process called worry. Realize again that worry is a prideful escape from Truth, from your own sense of failure. It is a selfish process whereby you are trying to prove your own goodness and evolve your own salvation as a noble god by saving your child. Playing god, you created the problem, but worrying is playing god again. In the process of worrying, you come up with all the wrong answers while emotionally projecting your identity as "god" into your child's mind.

God can't help while *you* are playing god. God cannot help your child while you are standing there, unholy in the place of the Holy, in his mind.

The answer is faith. Faith begins for you as soon as you are willing to realize the Truth about the game you have been playing. The Power Who gives, Who lives in this present moment of realization, is the same Who will, if you will let Him, save your child.

Let your child do his own suffering. Don't suffer for him or with him.

Resist the temptation to lose your own suffering in comforting his.

Do your own suffering.

Do you see how your suffering was eased by coming to the aid of your child, like an angel from heaven? Haven't

I said over and over again that the hell-nature in us comforts itself by inflicting suffering on others, even in the guise of helping?

As a tempter, you are as much addicted to the sin of comforting (playing god) as your victim is to the sin of being comforted. As long as this process continues, you will destroy one another without any hope of salvation. This is why I say, back off, butt out! Only when you realize the Truth that sets you free will the heavy burden and responsibility be lifted from your shoulders.

Of course, you feel responsible for what you have done. You have done a lot of harm playing god, and again in trying to solve "their" problems.

The cause may be external, but the cure is not. You got inside them; you did the damage, but *you* cannot repair the damage. Playing god did harm once, but trying to repair the harm is playing god again and again. Each time you responded to pressure, tried to help and failed, you suffered from guilt, from a greater and greater responsibility, which you stupidly turned around to mean you weren't being good enough, when it really should have meant: *butt out, stupid!*

How little faith you have! You respond to your child's cry as though there were nothing greater than you to answer it.

Do you want a miracle? Then realize what that heavy feeling of responsibility truly means in the Light of Reality. It simply means, dear lady, that you are responsible for playing god. Now, back off! Let your child be. Let him suffer his own suffering so he can grow up to be his own person.

Let him resent you for *not* coming to his rescue as has

been your custom. Resist the resentment candy bar of temptation, which, when it is changed to sorrow through guilt, makes you feel sorry enough for him to come out of "heaven" to help him, in order to make up for the guilt of resenting him. Resist the temptation of the little you in him, crying out to his "god," his mother. Both of you must now suffer through the pain of needs unanswered, and lo and behold—the awakening, the dawning of Truth for you and your beloved.

Do you want a big miracle? Then let it all begin with a little miracle of faith, the faith in God which is born of losing your own power to think up answers. There, beyond worry, is faith; the true way of knowing. The very Truth which makes you repent of playing god is God himself. Give your child over to this God.

Now let worry become concern. In concern, you cannot worry because you are above worry, realizing the lie of worry. Since you cannot be tempted to worry (and to answer) your pain remains a cry to the God that isn't you, Who comforts you in your suffering. Soon your child will be free from your worry, and you will no longer be the object of blame and the ongoing basis of his problem. He sees the Light of your innocence, your true concern. He sees love in you—not your love, but God's love. There's a difference. There is nothing more in you to blame or cry out to and the unanswered cry becomes a cry to be answered within himself. The problem is solved.

5: The Love That Causes Violence

Love anyone too much, and he will surely hate you. The main reason your children hate you is to stop your "loving." By tempting you to anger, they think they can find release from the possessiveness of your "love," from a terrible obligation they feel toward you—but this is an erroneous assumption which often backfires on them.

Shocked and threatened by your rebellious, ungrateful offspring, you respond with anger. As soon as your resentment subsides, you start feeling guilty, as though you had done something wrong—and you have! You are guilty of the cruelest form of mind control, concealed in a sugar-coating of love.

Resentment toward your children justifies you and temporarily distracts you from guilt. When guilt returns, you misconstrue it to mean that they are not grateful because you were not good enough to earn their homage. So you try harder to please (you manipulate) in order to be deserving of devotion. You put on a better performance but again are rejected. Now you are angry. In your self-righteousness, it is hard to realize why they are mistreating you. In reality, *you* are hurting *them*.

Their responses are part of a pattern of psychic self-defense to prevent you from "eating them alive" with the selfish, absorbing needs you foolishly believe to be love.

If true love were there behind your acts of self-sacrifice and kindness, there would be precious few problems you couldn't handle. A selfish motive is always revealed by your response of frustration (resentment) when you don't get results. The guilt of resentment, added to the guilt of seeking to be worshipped (vanity), accelerates into an ever-greater determination to make the infidels bend their knees. Because you are so steeped in pride, your only hope of (false) innocence rests in your worshipper's acceptance of you (as God). Your hardness of heart leads to frustration; it addicts you to a thankless, mindless treadmill, and often leads you eventually to disowning the "unworthy."

Guilt arises inexorably from selfish love, and resentment leads back again to guilt and whets the need to drench guilt in compulsive devotion. A vicious cycle!

Pride leads down into guilt, which expresses itself in many ways. One of them is an uncertainty about who or what you are, which develops into feelings of insecurity. The ego's attempt to be secure on its wobbly throne is the reason behind the craven need for worshippers, and that is what brings out hate, treachery and disrespect where you least expect to find it—in your own family.

The reason for the wretchedness of your existence should be getting clearer by now: you get involved with people for greedy, selfish reasons. You married, for example, seeking to "love away" some form of inferiority, insecurity and guilt inherited from your parents.

Our egotism and pride have come down to us by way

of the discourtesy, thoughtlessness and cruelty of our pathetic, devastated parents. Our souls are ravaged. Something is missing—you should know now that it is the relationship with God that has been lost through a weakness perhaps yet to be understood.

Instead of understanding its error and seeking to be reconciled to God, the corrupted identity seeks to gain the qualities it lacks *externally*, from the spirit of the corrupter as it reappears and embodies itself in other people. Our incompleteness then seeks to complete itself in the imperfect way, which is why we are drawn to opposite personalities. Females draw males, cowards draw bullies and the weak draw the strong.

A coward's need for courage draws him to the powerful, but instead of gaining courage by association, he actually loses what he has left. By association, the coward actually gives the bully the courage he is looking for, while becoming more fearful himself.

The psychotically fearful are like gamblers seeking riches and losing to the house. It is the gambler's riches that appear in the house; it is the slave's stolen strength that appears in the tyrant. So the house, our bullies and our lovers come to have more of the "riches" we are seeking and grow even more attractive and powerful. The evil power of all systems is built from the blood and guts of faithless sinners. We need what the house has and what bullies and lovers have; but when we try to beat the system or get our own back, we invariably fail. And when, in that failing, we try to identify with our idols to complete us, to become what they are and to acquire their character and nature, then we lose what little we had left.

There is an old saying: "If you can't lick 'em, join 'em." If you can't evolve their power in yourself through a fight, you seek to steal it in surrender.

The relationship of any beloved to his lover is similar to that interaction which should exist between man and his Creator. Man, the projection of God, is dependent on Him for all he is and ever will be. The little bit of God in each of us cries out for the ground of its being, to be nurtured and to grow more dependent on its Source. Such is the subservient, dependent relationship between the Divine Lover and His beloved.

When the divine relationship between God and man is severed by an emotional trauma and replaced by a similar but destructive alliance, we are divorced from wholeness and *in*-dependence to become the extension of the seducer. The implanted nature of the seducer in the victim cries out to evolve from a love-hate relationship with its creator. Until and unless it grows strong enough, by challenge and by contest, to overpower others, it can develop an identity only through surrender. The victim surrenders to gain the identity of the seducer, but pays for it with his substance. Under this system you can be brave, you can be rich and you can be powerful, but only by playing the same game with those weaker than yourself.

Capitulation to God makes you His extension and He rewards you with His sustaining love. He stamps you with His divine character. When you put another *person* on a pedestal, when you worship the glorious qualities he has, hoping to become like the object of your worship, you are bound to lose. This is the way all the parasites we idolize and identify with get their substance, their riches and power; the self-seeking masses are their nourishment. As virtuous people diminish and the "beautiful people" wax strong in power, civilization decays and falls.

There is tragedy ahead if you are trying to become one of those beautiful people to your family, for success can only be achieved at the expense of the crippled and the weak. Gutless or rebellious husbands, wives and children will be the result. Those most like you (those with greater egos) and also those with greater perceptiveness will see or sense their disadvantage and rebel. Thanks to them, you will at least have an opportunity to glimpse your folly before you drive the rebels to madness and suck the conformists completely dry.

To become an object of worship, you must baby another's ego. You must lift people's spirits with praise to newer, more glorious heights so that, in effect, you become their parent and their god. As the ground of their being, you emerge as the dominant factor. Once the victims descend from true grace to accept your homage, they are trapped; they devolve to exist on your loving reinforcement. You *must* sustain the ego you have created, or else you cannot hold that soul captive and satisfy your own lowly need for glory. You become so desperate to hold the reins of power that there is nothing you will not do to keep control—nothing!

In desperation and jealousy, you could kill your subjects rather than lose your "property." Every home with a loving, over-protective, demanding tyrant at its head is a potential Jonestown.

Rising to love another's need to be loved *just as he is* is tantamount to embodying the spirit of the ancient serpent in the Garden. With you, the legacy of evil continues; another Adam or Eve falls as pride evolves in its own conceit and in its dependence on hell's love to soothe away sin, and *you* receive the power. The victim can escape only to a familiar spirit. Men marry women just like their mothers—"out of the frying pan, into the fire."

Each emotional extreme is always the same; only *in the center* is there a true difference, rest and peace.

The principle here is that we cannot exist without completing ourselves by being joined to a ground of being, be it good or evil.

It is a female's miserable lot to be cast into the sustaining role of high priestess of hell's love. A woman practices this sick love on her menfolk, attempting to fulfill one of two mystical ancient needs. If she cannot find a woman's real fulfillment (correction through true love) she will bloat herself on her victim, encouraging his anger and his lust. The female's kingdom consists of helpless cripples —husbands and children, all driven mad with rebellion and conformity!

Bear in mind that dirty old devils and tyrants have needs too. To fulfill the need to be drunk with power, one must embody the spirit of corruption and, like it or not, drink in the stench of dying souls. Vampires and zombies are nourishment to one another, just as you and your lovers are! Under the spell of earthly love, people find ecstasy in sucking something from one another. Vampires are just as addicted to zombies as zombies are to vampires. Such is the nature of sensual loving and being loved.

Disenchantment with power causes a female to hiss with conceit and spit poison at her children and her husband like a venemous snake. She senses that her devoted, spineless subjects are somehow responsible for her agony—and, in part, they are. As reigning monarch, a woman spurns requests for favors, expressing contempt for even the smallest of demands, but she will purr with pleasure when offered tribute (only to become immediately discontented with it).

Through resentment, fear and frustration, and in your eagerness to please and to keep the peace, you will do more and more for such reigning monarchs while they do less and less for you. They will take everything you have and still not be satisfied.

This stubborn quality of pride passes from mother to child. It is mother who sets up her son to try to escape her, only to fall in love with her spirit in a younger female. The woman in the son cries out to complete "himself" in his wench. He surrenders to that which seems to be opposite to mother, but which is really just the same.

Your need to live and reign through your children can become so powerful that your identity, calling to you from your offspring, can literally suck up your "loving," sympathetic spirit into them, so that they can actually become you and you become them. Long before that time, there is a war, for the child's budding ego naturally tries to defeat the parent's purpose in every possible way.

What I am saying is that your child eventually becomes you in relationship to his own kids—or he is with you, period! He is full of secret hate or open contempt for his maker. Your child is first just a little projection of your wicked nature, but when he embodies you totally, you then feel the horror, the madness of his contempt and judgmental nature. Hate it, and you feed it the hate it needs to judge your judgment. Love it, and you sustain it as well—you can't win. Everything you feel, it feels and uses against you.

74

You once loved the son of "God" (your projection), but as that son nears the Godhead, you begin to fear and tremble. You despise him because he despises you and thinks himself to be greater than you. Guilt turns your loathing to loving and loving to loathing, and eventually all your strength oozes out of your body. Your creation reminds you of the ugliness of your pride and failing, which is another reason why you hate your children so.

Youngsters derive great pleasure from frustrating the selfish love-needs of their parents. It is common practice for them to abandon themselves "faithfully," lustfully to other lovers. They know only too well that you identify with them and that they are (an effigy of) you. They know *you* will feel every agony they can inflict upon themselves. They know their sins will be your sins. How they love to tarnish that beautiful image you have of yourself! Whatever happens to them also happens to you; what they feel, you also feel. So if they really want to pay you back for your failure, they only have to destroy themselves! It is all so easy. Hurting themselves is the same as getting to you; killing themselves can be like killing you! Of course, they could kill you too—"parenticide" is not that uncommon.

You fail to realize that the monster inside you crying for affection and company is nothing but a ravening beast, caring only as a lion does for its prey. In your pride, therefore, you *will not or cannot correct your children*— you can only corrupt them. What is corrected (loved) cannot provide a meal for the prideful beast within you.

Again, the secret motive behind worshiping someone is to trick him into seeing you in a greater light. It is the oldest trick in the world, upon which all evil is founded and comes into being.

Is that "someone special" your whole life? Then see him or her in a new light. See yourself as a smiling vampire whose existence hinges on your beloved's acts of false kindness. To get the world to revolve around you, you must lie-love; only then will the unwary surrender their souls. The weaklings who fall for it become addicted to receiving your vile rewards of approval, and they will see you as someone special, too. But those who are too aware are mercilessly punished for seeing you as you are.

Destruction is the devil's recreation. Each one of us has this terrible need to destroy others for our life. If there is none stout enough to stop us, we become addicted to destruction. The devastated victim inherits the destructive nature, and so is forced to destroy his destroyer or find his own victim if he is to survive. While youngsters naturally thrive on intrigue, if it goes unchecked and uncorrected, it can develop into a lust for life that can lead to murder and violence.

Sooner or later, in a right way or a wrong way, your children will assert their own individuality. Having evolved from your prideful nature, they usually do not have the grace to let the truth set them free. But they find bowing to your wishes intolerable. When the moment of revolt comes, those cute little things become transformed into unmanageable, ungrateful, mean brats and the battle is on. Their behavior becomes outrageous. Your patience is tried and found wanting and you are exposed as your world begins to crumble around you. What you do to make them mind, or to get them back, only drives them further away, more deeply into trouble. To get what each of you needs, you destroy each other. Each of you seeks the sweet pleasure of drawing first blood; that is to say, you try to get the other to respond emotionally with love or hate.

While they desperately need it and even demand it, one side of your children's natures fears true parental love and patience. Whether you are part of it or not, their budding egos will seek out and thrive on intrigue in their formative years. Brothers and sisters always fight like cats and dogs—if they don't, something is very wrong! As parents, you must *intercede* without becoming involved! Therefore, be just as stubborn in patience as they are in folly. Expect them to delight in diluting your parental authority and getting away with murder (yours, if they can). Do not let them be the death of you. Persist with firm, no-nonsense, patient love. *Give them the opportunity to glimpse their folly so that correction might originate from the authority of their own conscience.* Incidentally, that is the goal of true love. Your unwavering patience is the *electric* example they need. When that kind of impression gets inside them, it wars with and drives out the sin of pride.

There is a world of difference, you see, between internally and externally induced guilt. The former reconciles a person with the God of his conscience, while the latter reconciles him to a *person-god,* which induces a fresh guilt...and rage...and guilt. Then he is bound to go back again to the sin of reconciling to a personality god who rewards him with the "redeeming" horror of loving him as he is.

When love is dispassionate, pride is set aside and you are not selfishly involved. No judgments are made, you give no approval. The hostile one now can find nothing wicked or greedy in you to distract, justify or comfort him, and thus is forced to encounter himself.

When your beloved cannot destroy your patience, when something deep within you glows even brighter when he tries, the light coming through awakens him to God within himself. *The cure of all human ills and suffering lies in inducing this encounter, this conflict with the true self.*

Playing the god game, your ego can never be happy until others come crawling on their bended knees, begging forgiveness and love. Again, your happiness must turn to grief because, after they have received your "grace," you find your love has done nothing but condoned more evil. And in the process, you have created in them a greater need for the services of "Your Highness of Forgiveness."

For heaven's sake, before it is too late, realize that *you have no redemptive power to change anyone for the good.* Your vanity has nothing but the power to frustrate by your sympathizing with what has already become rotten in your beloved. Sick love makes sick people, and in that sickness they crave the love that makes them even sicker. When they get it, they will hate you for it; that is your frustration. When your love violates, it sows violence, and your dilemma is just payment for your supreme folly.

You and the extension of you, your counterpart, are selfishly entangled with each another. You take something—his life substance; you give something—an identity that flowers and builds from you, one which loves and hates and, like you, destroys others for its survival.

Selfish people make demands, and the "selfless" give and sacrifice until there is nothing left to give. They run, they rebel, they die to others. Just as long as you are stubborn about pride, wanting to be right and never wrong, to that degree you are addicted to the horror of either chasing your loved ones into hell, or drawing them toward it. Both slave and tyrant fear freedom from each other because *where freedom is, there also is the truth* about what a pair of creeps they have become!

When you are emotionally involved with other people, you cannot grow spiritually as you should. Therefore, love unselfishly. Let them go. Give up those cozy, warm feelings you want from them. Love and shake your children loose. Observe the folly of *feeling-based love.* Discover the true life-experience that arises just behind that selfish, sensuous feeling.

Little egos can deal with selfishness, in a way. Everything that is wrong with them nourishes itself from it. The farther apart you are emotionally from your children, the closer you come together with a spirit of divine love. With true love you find yourself alone, distant from the flesh, but closer to the Reality that created you both.

Through being less angry and less "nice," you become a formidable enemy and a good friend. It becomes easy to deny the selfish luxury of helping others, because wisdom forbids it. True love knows that ill-timed help can hurt and cripple.

Expect nothing from anyone and you will not be frustrated or disappointed. *Children have no love to give; they are much more likely to betray your trust, even in the smallest things.* But their consciousness is raised by your contrast, and they do recognize a love-authority when love is present. Brace yourself for difficult times and remember to be *patient.* For their sake, set aside your ego-emotional need to hate; by this means, their offense will be directed against themselves and not against you.

Even adults will sometimes cheat you, hoping against hope that you can meet their unfulfilled need for correction. They may not be bad. It is just that inside them is a naughty child who never grew up. They may actually be seeking to experience the special embarrassment that can save them, which your awareness fosters.

A loving parent does not prematurely reward his children with too much too soon; he allows good things to come independently, in the Creator's own special time. Love is not a grace-robber.

One way to enslave an executive is to pay him more than he is worth. This sort of false, premature recognition puffs up his pride and addicts him to money and to the intelligence behind it. Because he tasted the reward before he was worthy, his *independence*, the magic of arriving at those rewards through discipline of character, is destroyed. From that point on, he is obliged to sacrifice his principles to hold on to the kingly luxuries his ego has descended to need.

Beware of the friend/fiend. As I have said before, children are rarely motivated by anything but selfish gain and an assortment of appeals to their egos. They must be protected from those who can steal their affection with false, enslaving "generosity." Protecting your children from benevolent parasites is a thankless task. It appears to them that you are separating them from the fulfillment of real needs and from well-deserved recognition; they may protest that you are denying them their freedom or even their human rights.

Protect them but don't overprotect. Overprotecting is

tantamount to guarding a meal to keep other vultures from eating it. Kids know that and hate you for it. They may escape and get eaten just to spite you, and then you will lament (not for them, but for your lost meal).

Don't fret too much. The games youngsters play— cops and robbers, slave-tyrant intrigues, and all the lying and excuse-making are part of growing up. While they need intrigue, don't you provide it. Stand in contrast; it will be their salvation. If they did not grow from being cute little devils into big, selfish pigs, they would hardly grow at all. *Only if you are unlike them can you help them to see and transcend their selfish natures.*

It is imperative that the childish ego, with its needs and greeds, grow toward the threshold of realizing what it has become. If you become part of the fight, you cannot be the referee. If you are the spectator, you cannot be the referee. So do not become emotionally involved, and do not become disinterested; instead, you must be *unemotionally involved.*

Do not be impatient with your children's imperfections. Do not condition them with fear and anger. Do not repress them or motivate them to act like saints. If it takes five years for them to realize the value of brushing their teeth, then let it take five years. I know you could condition them to do it in five minutes, but then you would have a creature of conditioning rather than a person.

When your children are small, you inadvertently contribute to their ego growth by hugging and kissing them. Then comes the time when you must stand in contrast. Children naturally grow beyond the hugging and kissing need. It is mother, for the most part, who provides for the ego growth; it is father's job to take over and stand in corrective contrast. Mothers build egos; fathers help children transcend them. Believe me, it takes a real man to see the children through, and he must be very strong in faith.

By now you should have identified your own weakness.

Adults are, for the most part, overgrown children. As your ego-self develops through pride and approaches the threshold of reality, you should begin to realize that you must transcend childish love, hate and excitement as sources of security and motivation. You parents have experienced the conflict that is produced by a lifetime of emotional intrigue long before your children do, and so you can understand and come to grips with your children's lusts before they can even recognize the danger.

Children thrive on the very emotions that cause conflict in the mature adult. Understanding can lead to emotional maturity if we welcome it—but usually we do not. Instead, a glimpse of truth more often drives people into a second emotional childhood. The average soul is ill-prepared to encounter reality. Because we grew up uncorrected, without loving parents, our sins have made most of us too guilty to face reality as a friend.

Just as awakening to our own inner reality threatens our sinning soul and drives us further into our own emotionality, so do awareness and honesty outside us, in our seeking children, compel us to emotionalize them. More parents than you can shake a stick at resent and fear the (relative) innocence of their children. The guilty cannot stand being observed. Their children's acute perception seems to persecute them like an evil eye, and they respond emotionally, defensively, to put out the light— which to them is painful, and therefore wicked. A child reflects the mood of his parents and when they succeed in emotionally disturbing him, the limelight is focused on the "sick" child rather than on the real culprits. The guilty always strive to conceal themselves by making the innocent out to be evil.

Realize that your parents were never given understanding and love. Even parents need true love. For this cause, dear children, you can resolve your resentment against your parents. They are not persecuting you at all; it is your emerging consciousness that is really persecuting *them*. Part of them wants you to hate them to justify its own wickedness. If their souls are still alive, they need to encounter your patience to help them experience the relief of redeeming shame. Don't let the light go out by nursing your resentment. *You are old enough to "father" your own parents.* Grace them with the chance to experience themselves. Now when they persecute you, meet them *with innocence, with patience and long-suffering.* Overcome evil with good!

Outgrow selfish love and hate. Be objective, distant; grow emotionally mature, fulfilled beyond the old Satan-game of love and hate.

Parents, stand back from the back-biting intrigues arising from childish thoughtlessness. Remember that emotionality tempts a child to reflect the hell of your pride, causing both of you to grow in conflict—with yourselves and with one another.

Be unselfish. Be strong—strong enough to abandon the security of approval. Also stop thriving on hate. Deny yourself the luxury of love and hate, and save their souls, to save your own!

Be neutral. Maintain a healthy, objective distance from

your beloved children. Across this gap no evil can pass from you or to you. Then you cannot tempt your children, neither can they tempt you. You cannot fulfill your ego needs from them and they cannot gratify themselves on you. You become free from one another to embrace your common Father in heaven and to grow from the ground of your own individual being.

People will try your patience. When you observe what is wrong with people, it is only human nature for them to turn things around defensively to seem as if there were something wrong with *you* for seeing it. That is the way guilty people react when they are observed. They survive in their wrong by making you doubt yourself. Even when they are caught "red-handed," you are called the liar, the bad guy, the one in a bad mood. It is the same with apprehended criminals: the police are the culprits. So stay calm. Love in the moment by not resenting (by being distant) in the moment. Observe. Abandon the secret resentment; let it pass. Free your children from the agony of judging your judgment, once and for all; don't give their judgment of you a leg to stand on.

Take your children's poison, neutralize it and change it into love! Don't allow yourself to be changed and poisoned, or you will lose the power to change things for the better!

Don't give or accept false love.

Don't hate or thrive on being hated.

Look at your need for security as weak and selfish, and all at once that insecurity will become the security you have always sought.

Life is an on-going battle. You are involved in good fighting or in bad fighting. You must fight *for,* not against your children. Fight calmly in your stand for what is just. Feel pain but not guilt. Suffer through betrayal and agony; you must endure such trials without resentment. All parents, good ones or bad ones, must suffer at the hands of their own children. Children must observe their parents hurting *but never hating*, always cheerful, never bitter, always getting better. If you are getting worse, they will hate you, because it means they must become worse, too. Your failure to love and endure excites and pleases the sick nature, freeing the soul from the guilt of what it has done, liberating it to sin again.

Failure tempts; patience repents.

Many parents who have terrible resentment against their children's outrages become self-made martyrs who learn to enjoy their own suffering, reveling in their hatred and judgment. Failing that, they become child-persecutors. For such as these who wish to remain in ignorance, there is no hope. They have engineered their own tragedy and that of their children.

Children, you can escape such parents by having compassion for them instead of hating them. And you can escape by seeing how the compulsive "love" you may feel for them is only born of a need for approval and of guilt for what you secretly feel because of what they have done to you.

Be prepared to suffer, either for the sake of righteousness or for unrighteousness. It is far better to suffer for righteousness' sake. It profits one *little* to suffer well-deserved punishment, but suffering for what is *just* and right reveals the secret of life. Again, seek no security, no love, no hate—seek only the security of truth.

Only through patiently suffering the pain of many years

of betrayals and persecutions without a cause can you help your persecutors, especially your own family members, to realize salvation. It is your own evolving consciousness that makes others aware of what they are doing to you and to themselves. They see your grace, your aloneness in the world. They see your strength, rooted in an invisible ground of being, and they are profoundly impressed.

6: Discipline

Funny thing about people—if you leave them alone to be free, they take liberties; they become wild and ruthless. Then, when they force you to lay down the law in order that society may survive, you (the rule maker) become a despotic tyrant. This principle marks the beginning and the end of all relationships and of all cultures—it's just a matter of time. The only variable is how much time it takes.

You must seek the way that is truly FREE. Through God's grace you must become as one who can never be ruled, simply because you don't need law. You must become as one who cannot be seduced to rule. You must become one who can breed this marvelous quality of freedom in your family. For without grace, a person is led to the many lawless freedoms that eventually demand restraint, and the spirit that leads to all these false freedoms rises from the pit as a reformer. Only one who is perfectly free has the authority to set others perfectly free from that prison system of law and lawlessness.

Since the beginning, the oppressed have carried within them the natures of their oppressors. All cowards are bullies: strong before the weak, weak before the strong. The "weak" in your case are your children. Before them, it is safe to be mighty.

You carry into marriage the temptations of the past, with its "karma" of misery and suffering. The plan for the soul's salvation is in the Light (where meditation brings you). The secret of the law of Light is patience. The soul living in the Light, never being intimidated and never intimidating, is saved.

The patient soul does not respond, nor does it cause others to respond. Patience never fails, nor does it cause others to stumble. Not submitting, it not only cannot give up power, but it takes (wrong) power and authority away. All the valleys are raised and all the hills are lowered—all become equaled before the Light.

Look now at the lifestyle you have inherited, and look ahead to what you are compelled to project (impatiently) to your offspring. Therefore, have compassion upon your children; free them from this loathsome legacy of sin and death.

Let me tell you more: your impatience is born of pride. It stimulates others to grow pridefully—first as psychotic subjects of their "creator" and later on as carriers; infectious, impatient, prideful perpetuators of the sin of pride.

The authority to pass on the military chain gang of pride lies as much with the victim as with the cruel tyrant. Tyrants beget tyrants, and tyrants also produce slaves. Slaves create carbon copies of themselves as well as their own opposites. I tell you truly that a boy can really hate the mother who sees no wrong in him. When she caters to his ego, the child's soul puffs up with the madness of conceit and takes advantage. Out of anger and fear of violence towards her, he can also suppress his emotions into submission—to become a slave appeasing a sweet Hitler.

Therefore, just as you must not be impatient, neither should you appease impatience. Never appease your children, your wife or anyone. You would never feel the need to appease if you didn't feel pressure. Less and less pressure is felt as you grow in patience and in grace, as you refrain from responding with resentment and pride. Through the medium of your impatience, pride projects through the medium of the victim's resentment, setting up the system of slaves and tyrants. You carry the seed to become one or the other.

Protect your children from tyrants who try to enslave them, and from the sticky-sweet ones who will spoil them rotten and then raise them up as private love-hate objects.

Protect them against the patronizing mother—and from the patronizing father who has become a mother.

Protect them against the violent, manly woman.

Protect them against friends who look up to them and comfort them—and friends who humiliate them.

Make no mechanical rules. Use your God-given wisdom and strength to keep them secure from the many subtle ego appeals, manipulations and pressures of the dog-eat-dog system of pride. Talk to them about what is happening around them.

Subject them mostly to the *cleaving edge* of your love, the love that keeps them from being entangled with the world, the love that neutralizes pride because it is not proud. If you can keep them from the evil force with your good force, then they will one day experience your kind of freedom.

The good force does nothing but cancel out the sick suggestions of the world, leaving your child free to realize the true path for himself. If any child is protected by such persistent love as this, the chances are he will eventually begin to choose the right way over the wrong, the way that never takes advantage, and of which no one can take advantage.

If all men and women were to be free like this, we would have a world with no rulers and no followers—a world where suffering would no longer exist, and God's unfolding plan and glory would everywhere be seen. Governments would be reduced to administrations of God's Kingdom-on-earth as it is in Heaven.

Therefore, take hold of faith and, with patience, *love*.

Love does not spank a small child simply because he "won't mind" or because he is forever getting into everything. It is evil to condition a baby against danger with anger or fear.

Constant vigilance is your parental duty. A lapse of consciousness (yapping on the telephone with a friend, for example) can leave your child to drown, to get run over by a car or the like. Your love is represented by awareness. Your awareness is your child's protection until the day his own awareness begins gradually to take over.

Children naturally take up a lot of your time, a big chunk of your life, but give it willingly and not grudgingly. Be careful not to resent those imagined restrictions of your "freedoms," or the demands on your time. Give the time demanded of you patiently, dutifully and unselfishly, and the good Lord will then extend His eternal time to you. Learn to be patient, observe, and so resolve your willfulness in favor of what is just. The naughty child in you, who never knew parental love, will grow to become a parent with love.

Patience is the panacea for all human ills. Patience "teaches" good to others, just as impatience teaches violence. Patience awakens and raises the consciousness, just as impatience lowers the consciousness into dreams —and into slavery.

Love never pushes children toward anything, whether potty-training or schooling. If you have to remind them ten thousand times to do such things as clean their teeth, then do so. Do everything patiently and persistently until they grow to see the value of any discipline for themselves. Surely you don't want to develop robots or rebels, do you? Then don't scream and holler, rant and rave, push and pressure, or otherwise set them up to answer to that sort of authority later on in life. Make them aware through being aware yourself—through patience. Responding with their own growing awareness, they will one day come to recognize their responsibility and take over your job. They will be newly respectful toward your vigilance and care.

However, if you fail, if you push and pressure, they will rebel and, through pressure or neglect, grow wild and undisciplined—with obvious consequences. You will be troubled and constantly worried wherever they go, knowing deep down inside that they are not protected by the spirit of understanding which every human being ought to carry with him. You may live in fear that something bad will happen, and you will be tormented by fear. *Your* mind (you in them) may be with them wherever they go, but that sort of low-grade awareness cannot protect them, simply because you are not God. Your fear for them may be picked up and become translated into their own fear for themselves. Your children can become insecure, dependent on others for "protection" and, in the end, they will be victimized by those in whom they put their trust.

You will experience your children's pain, their suffering—even their failings—as your own. You put your failing spirit into them through pressure and life-long impatience (hatred). You have pain because your conscience pricks your pride into awakening regarding the failing of that kind of "protection"—but you resent it. You cannot hurt another without suffering what they suffer. Such a sin is as often one of *omission* as of commission. Failure to love *hurts,* and you feel the torments of your victim. Your failure to love anyone is your failure to save them —and to save yourself.

You owe your child love, and one aspect of love is protection—protection from your own weakness or wickedness, through patience, and protection from the cruel, violent, seductive and impatient world.

Protect your child even from your own parents if need be. Don't allow your parents to lay on your kids what they did to you. If you have very stubborn, sick parents, the best thing to do is to get far away and live in a private world with your own little family. (Careful! Don't be paranoid about this.) You may even have to protect your child against a mate—a weak, patronizing, or over-strict husband perhaps. For your child's well-being, you may have to separate. But the biggest danger is that you, the defender of the faith, could be the psychotic parasite who is destroying your own child. You could hypocritically turn Truth around and, with a jaundiced eye, use it against the good soul who is trying to protect your child against *you*. (Beware! There are counterfeit meditators, just as there are counterfeit Christians.)

Above all, watch out for the vile school system. Carefully monitor your child's emotional state when he comes in from school. Make sure the child is not being pressured and degraded by an impatient teacher. The chances are that your child will be singled out for persecution and destruction if he is aware and naturally bright. Be strong with the principal and the teachers. Give fair warning to all teachers that you want your child *exposed* to information, but you don't want knowledge shoved down his throat. Let the teachers know, in no uncertain terms, that you will daily shove *your* demands down *their* throats (so to speak) by your "obnoxious" presence, if they start their monkey business. Give them some of their own medicine. If "it's right to pressure" your kids, then they shouldn't mind your pressuring them, should they? But do it with the strength which comes from knowing what is right, without the threat factor of resentment.

Better still, keep your child *out* of public school as long as it is legally feasible and, if at all possible, start your own school with a few other sensitive, seeking people. Children learn better later, when they are older, and develop their own natural curiosity. What is more, *a non-corrupted child will teach himself better than any teacher can.*

Once a child has been corrupted through pressure, he loses touch with his inner reality. He therefore has to be motivated—which is the very excuse the motivators use to go on pressuring your child. But if you let him recover, you won't believe your eyes.

Schools have always been very, very sick indeed, but

never as bad as today. Children are committing suicide by the thousands every year, even eight and nine-year-olds. The cause is a combination of parental and school pressure. Children are squeezed, without protection, between these two forces.

All violence against teachers is actually a turn-around of the generations of violence against children, against unspoken, invisible destruction. Schoolteachers (and parents) have for years been secretly murdering children with their impatient pressures, in the name of Good, God and Country!

The kind of insane bureaucrat who runs your local school/prison system does it for feelings of importance and power, rarely for what is good for kids. This kind will *never ever* admit they are wrong. They actually enjoy hurting. Even though kids are burning down schools, mugging and killing teachers, one another and themselves, school boards press on regardless, ignoring the facts, trying new approaches to "education."

Children are being systematically destroyed mentally, emotionally and physically, by parent-school pressures. Parents are often as oblivious to what they are doing to their children as the schoolteachers are. Why is this so, you ask? Because of PRIDE. Through pride, they have become blind, unaware zombies, powerless to prevent even their own destruction under the system.

Pride can never be wrong. The prideful dare not recognize any other way except their own. There is only one way for egomaniacs, and "their" way must be the only way no matter who dies or who must suffer. They are oblivious to the harm they inflict because they hate the truth, especially the truth of their own wickedness and failing, which they are compelled to pass on in order to relieve their own suffering. Hurting others has a strange way of relieving hurt, temporarily.

If you give your spiritual and educational responsibilities over to other people, it shows you don't love your children. If you really had love, you would see where that responsibility lies. If you had love, you would see the danger of delivering youngsters into the hands of blood-sucking ministers, Sunday School teachers, or any other sort of babysitter. Those who are eager to do this job for you are usually birds of prey, waiting for the likes of you to abandon your nest.

Don't ever leave your children with a babysitter unless he or she is extremely well-known to you and your child. You wouldn't believe the terrible (even sexual) abominations babysitters commit with a weak, helpless child when no one is around.

Face it: you are stuck in the role of parent. Your sexual need (a form of ego-selfishness) has trapped you. Now it is time to overcome your willful, self-seeking, roving mind. Stop hating the drudgery of being home, washing diapers and dishes; stop wishing you were somewhere else, doing something more "rewarding" and ego-gratifying. Learn to be a real, committed human being with your family. There is endless joy in learning to be a parent. The salvation of your soul is at stake—even eternal life.

Do you realize that if you had been a whole human being in the first place, you might not have found yourself as an inadequate (perhaps single) parent in the second place? Your sin, your lack of wholeness, your prideful, greedy need to gratify the lust to be complete, is what drove you into the false fulfillment of sex. The fusion of a man to a woman is not *and never can be* real love; it's just two selfish egos sucking on each other's life. That selfish urge, and the eventual use of another person to gratify your pride, traps you resentfully, even if too eagerly, into marriage, the master/slave relationship. And the trap closes tighter when a child appears.

Having become a slave through greed, use and abuse, chances are your ego resents all restrictions on your freedom. But those who do look forward to being parents are not as loving as they appear—they usually have selfish motives, too. Some women want to live their lives through a baby subject of their very own. They want to make good their failing at the hands of their *own* vampirish parents. A child offers the opportunity for parents to regain stature, to look good (like God) through prideful and willful maneuvers with their offspring, so that the parent's ego can proudly proclaim to the world, "Look how marvelous I am! I'm not so bad. I'm not a failure because, look, I have made my child into a success..." On the other hand, the same wicked spirit can achieve the same deceptive sense of success in the opposite way, by downgrading and confusing a child so that, by comparison to the *child's* failing, the parent can seem superior. False glory and self-righteousness are what you seek, and if you seem devoted to your child, it is only because you need him to attain that end.

Every person who is spoiled by impatience and pressure becomes a victim. Not knowing the true way to salvation, he becomes right and superior by creating another victim. He lives through his victim, or in contrast to his victim. The pride can find comfort in comparing itself to those less fortunate, or in being responsible for (and involving itself with) another's greatness.

Let us say that your selfish parents spoiled you rotten and weakened you to depend on their false kindness and generosity, because it made them feel good and superior to be able to do such a thing. If you rebelled, the pain of failing to rebel creatively has followed you around and, perhaps, forced you to find a victim of your own. Now you are like your parent. At this point the only way to *not* feel like a victim is to victimize. It may not be the real cure, but it *feels* good; it *seems* as though it is the cure. That is why few parents can see the harm they do when they spoil, or otherwise demoralize their children with overt acts of cruelty. *Sick parents feel good whether spoiling or degrading their children.*

Did your parents spoil you? If so and you are a woman, you could find yourself being too sympathetic to your boyfriend or your husband to obtain a needed superior feeling. For his need to feel superior, a man who has been spoiled usually will look for opportunities to take advantage of others and, in general, will act like the ungrateful, rebellious child he was to his parents. Through her "generosity" a woman may end up so hurt, so destitute, that she could be forced to go back and depend on the doting, indulgent parents she despises, yet now needs. Spoiled children always need their parents but they also hate them for helping them, because their help has hurt and weakened them. We are trapped in a system where our parents subtly degrade us and make themselves seem like beautiful beings from Heaven, while slowly strangling the life out of us.

See how complicated it all is—yet how simple? The lesson is this: if you must depend on someone, gracious or not, get your pride out of the way. Never be humiliated. Take gifts graciously, or don't accept them at all. However, refusing aid when you need help can be as much an act of pride as taking. Wherever pride is involved, you will feel guilty. Can you see how you can be weakened by taking as well as by not accepting when you need it? We all need help at times, and one must learn to give with grace as well as to receive graciously. While it is indeed better to give than to receive, without receivers there can be no givers. Gracious receiving allows gracious giving. And even where giving is not gracious, you may learn to defeat the humiliation by receiving graciously if you will, without resentment.

Do you identify with all this? Doesn't this explain the behavior of your own children, in the light of your apparent kindness? If you have real understanding of what love is, then you can never be victimized by "love" or hate, or by the process of giving and denying. And, not being a victim, it will not be in you to victimize. The ancient curse will be broken.

It is also cruel to buy a child's love and affection. Never compensate with material things to make up for your impatience, for your failure to be ever-present with them. Ambition, impatience and absence can make you feel guilty and can cause you to bestow character-weakening favors and advantages, preventing your children from growing up fully able to provide for themselves.

The finest heritage you can pass on to your children is the virtue of *in*-dependence—as opposed to *out*-dependence. Independence comes through the exercise of self-denial, money disciplines, sound judgment and investment. The knowledge that they can provide for themselves, being beholden to no one, is the basis of true confidence and freedom.

Never justify your ambition for money (which keeps you away from home) by telling your family you are doing it all for them! That is a lie and you know it. Ambition draws you out of the home, frustrates you and makes you impatient; then impatience leads you back to ambition. Try to remember what I have said many times before: pride always leads to prideful emotion and emotion must always lead back to the reinforcement of all aspects of pride—and to conflict with family and self.

It is good to let your children suffer from little errors of judgment. Never feel sorry for them; never comfort them unduly. For example, if they have spent their money impulsively and they want you to lend them money to buy this or that, it's better for them that you say, "No"—*with an explanation.* As they grow older, encourage them to consult with you before making decisions about buying cars or dating girls. If you see them poised to make a deadly mistake, don't be afraid to be strong about what you see. A twenty-five-year-old is as blind as a bat when it comes to such things as sexual infatuation.

Wherever possible, it should always be the father who admonishes the children. A sensible wife should stand back and let him do his thing *without her support. Her support always weakens his case! A real man never ever needs any backing from a woman.* There is no poison worse for a child than to hear the background cackle of his "amen-ing" mother when his father is trying to straighten him out! *A woman's support ruins a man's correction.* The correct thing for a man to do under those circumstances is to turn his attention away from the problem with his child and admonish his wife. Having taken care of her, he can then turn back to correcting his child *all by himself.* Furthermore, it is even worse for a man to side with his wife against the children!

A man must be careful when correcting his wife and children. While seeking souls more often than not welcome loving correction, unseeking people really hate it with a passion. If you have one of these incorrigible wives or kids, watch out! They will misconstrue your intention to restrain them for their own good and get you into trouble with the law. Watch out for that trap. Only your intuition can protect you and show you just who is who. And be careful you are not a hypocrite using this text to recapture your prey.

You must know whom to help and whom not to help. Your own salvation rests squarely on knowing the difference. You must be sincere in order to recognize the difference, and you must be sincere in order to have the strength to take the correct course and follow it to its ultimate conclusion. Test to know the difference. A woman can put up a good fight to test the persistence of your love!

As you must see, all true knowledge is revealed in mystery, and *no pretender or fake meditator* can ever cross this border to save children, wives or husbands; to have happiness and, eventually, eternal life. They will all fail by not going far enough, or by going too far.

It is sheer folly to praise or to condemn your children. Praising builds egos into conflict; so does condemning them. Never think for one moment that condemning diminishes pride one bit, for it does just the opposite, swelling a child's pride through his secret resentment and judgment.

Once corrupted by praise, children often become addicts. Because praise actually seduces, corrupts and weakens children, they develop a lower and lower sense of self-worth. Addicted to praise, they will literally sell their minds and souls for it. Praise, like all its cousins (music, drugs, alcohol, etc.), actually lowers their worth under the *pretext* of raising the spirit, because of what they must lower themselves to do to obtain it (praise).

Guilt associated with praise may drive its victims to seek condemnation. They begin to fear success and unconsciously make silly mistakes to make you mad, hoping to get you to neutralize the pain caused by your approval. Of course, that could cause you to think you are not praising them enough. Plenty of trouble here! You may drive them out to seek lowly company, people who will degrade them, in the hope that degradation will release them from the pain of your love and positive thinking.

Alas, on either end there are agonies of swollen pride. The cruelty of degradation then could drive them back to the cruelty of praise, until one day they become afraid of making changes and get stuck in a rut as permanent victims of praise or of condemnation. The pain could make them want to shoot themselves and all those who are involved in love/hate games of praise and condemnation.

So, acknowledge good performance, but never praise it. Acknowledge bad performance, but don't condemn it. There must never be condemning or condoning in your words—no emotion or exaggeration of pleasure or of displeasure. If your child draws a good picture and shows it to you for comment, appraise it honestly without emotion. Give your honest opinion. Is it quite good? Then say so calmly. Don't pump up the child's ego by emotion-charged exclamations of "Magnificent!" and "Wow, you are going to be a great artist!" (You could get them hung up on an artist's trip when they have no talent.) If the work could stand improvement, then you might do well to ask your child if he welcomes constructive criticism. Chances are, you will receive the go-ahead and then gentle criticism will be welcomed and taken under serious consideration.

As I said before, it is *reaction* that sets up in you the nature of your corruptor. You inherit his way of corrupting others through emotionally-loaded praises and condemnations. Now you fall under a compulsion to praise or to damn, to be praised or to be damned. Either approach breaks down the character of the victim, feeding the transplanted demons within. Corruption is the way of life for "demons," who feed on your fluctuations between being super "nice" and super cruel. That patronizing "nice" is not so nice.

Evil has both a "nice" and a cruel side, just as good does. Evil weakens with "niceness" and weakens with cruelty. Good strengthens with its goodness and again strengthens with what "hurts," because it helps. Evil "corrects" you when you are right, or praises you for being right, accepting and praising you *until* you become wrong, and again when you *are* wrong. It's terribly confusing—unless, of course, you are in your center.

It's all in your attitude. Love knows that fine line of difference between acknowledgement and praise, between correcting and condemning. Because love knows the difference, love begets a child of love, free from the conditionings of the world.

7: A Force Called Love

Most women do not realize the harm they do to their children by resisting a man's good-natured correction—that is, if they are lucky enough to be married to a halfway decent man. And men rarely realize the harm they do by failing to give correction—not having any real love to give.

The essence of true love is not billing and cooing and being nice and friendly; it is correction. Correction is the love we all need but is also what many of us fear. Great wisdom and superb strength are needed to correct errant behavior. The basic principle to realize is that love is a facet of understanding which reveals itself in justice and in strength.

First, love is patient. Without patience, everything you say or do will be wrong.

Second, the effect of your love is not your responsibility. You may see the need to point out errors or faults to another, but you are not responsible for whether or not they accept your correction. It is relieving to know that you personally are never responsible for change in another. Your pride must never be involved. The determination of your individual responsibility depends upon the relationship you have, whether it is with your wife, husband, child, friend, stranger or employer.

Third, love may be silent. Bear in mind that silent corrections are just as potent as verbal ones. The right kind of silence at the right time, the right kind of look with perfect timing has powerful, meaningful impact. (By correction, I mean standing as a patient, long-suffering example of what another should *be* and *see* in himself.)

To understand why you must be patient (non-responsive), you need to know the true nature of man:

People were not created to take shape from emotional pressure. The Divine Will and Purpose, expressing Itself through the pressure of conscience, must be the order of life. It is only natural to try to rebel against outrageous authority. Since most children cannot rebel successfully, they end up conforming to pressure and expressing the will behind the pressure. Then they become addicted to pressure and unable to function from within. While some children appear to behave like angels in the presence of authority, they revert back to worse mischief "when the cat's away." Outwardly, they are models of good behavior but inwardly they are like what their Bible-thumping, over-strict parents are inside—straining at the leash.

Pressure develops two extreme evils, only one of which I have discussed. The other extreme is a totally rebellious creature, nothing like his phony, pushy parents on the outside. Instead, he is *outwardly* like what they are *inside*—in every respect.

Only ambitious, sick, demented, guilt-ridden parents will push their offspring to learn, to be religious, to succeed in anything. The confounded parent, himself the product of false education and pressure, has little tolerance for childish innocence and selfhood.

Unfortunately, once you have become infected through parental pressure, religious pressure, school pressure, etc., you take on the vile, impatient spirit behind the pressure. The usual defense against the rape of the mind is resentment. Through resentment, children try to block the intent of the "mind bender," but the spirit in the parent knows the child's resentment will work in its favor. All the child can block, if anything, is the religion or the learning—not the invasion of the spirit.

Some children stop learning in an attempt to preserve their own identity, to be themselves. Those who go on to become bright achievers have exactly the same identity problem but are unable to keep out the knowledge. They become mere carbon copies. The inferiority and guilt of not being himself drives this type of child to compensate; he egotistically justifies his servitude through the possession of knowledge he is too weak to reject.

So, while one child may be cast in the parental mold, the other appears to be the opposite, the outcast, the "black sheep" of the family. The black sheep may be a drunk or a drug addict. He is sick or very, very emotionally ill. Whatever is wrong, the outcast obviously needs treatment. Everyone looks down on him, or they are sorry for him and try to "help."

There is nothing worse than being "helped" by the very sort who destroyed you in the first place. Resenting that "help" is another futile attempt to reject it but, as you know, that only lets the destruction in. This "help" is an evil concern for its own transplanted kind; it is also a way of finishing off and sowing confusion in any soul who will not surrender. That one is spiritually, psychologically, and emotionally murdered.

Do you see why I have related all of this? You most likely identify with one side of the problem or the other. If so, we are communicating. Now I want to reveal how delicate your approach must be with your children. Your wife, sir, was no doubt a victim of this sort of tortured past and "it" in her is having "its" way through you and your children. You must be careful of your emotional reaction. Remember how resentment works for "it" and against you.

"It" is what you must deal with in yourself before you can cope with "it" outside you, and inside others. "It" in you cannot constructively cope with "it" in others. Perhaps you already see that. Remember, one "it" always plays the tyrant and another "it" plays the slave who, through resentment, grows up from the relationship with the tyrant. The slave is hoping, of course, to evolve in his own right and become a tyrant; that is the reason for his submission. *"It" patterns itself after the parent and this fact manifests itself with children.* (It is important to point out here that "it" is a big coward and that you only need to have faith in what you know is right and "it" will run scared.)

You must learn to look at "it" in yourself calmly, without resenting what you see. That is how "it" will begin to die; and that, too, is how the real you will be born and begin to flower. Remember, any kind of resentment strengthens the "it" nature, especially resentment against it in yourself. "It" in you thrives and grows from your resentment against the parent (or mate) in yourself, even as "it" did when "it" lived in your parent. "It" inside you teases you to resent "it," so that "it" can continue to feed on your energies and drive you into a psychotic state, or to live "its" life through you.

After you have looked at "it" in you, you must look quietly at "it" in your rebellious wife to make sure you don't resent her, to make sure her "it" doesn't grow up in you as a slave to her. Remember, as a rebel, "it" thrives on emotional reaction, impatience and any form of tease or intimidation. That rebellious spirit in your wife might cause her to see in you—even promote in you—the father or mother she enjoyed hating in her childhood. Even true innocence can threaten that willful, wifely "it" into becoming very excited and agitated, trying to make you think you are doing something wrong even when you are right. The motive is to weaken you and make you doubt yourself, to make you violent so as to have "its" way. "It" needs you to play the weak (or violent) role of the hated parent; otherwise, "it" cannot survive. Like "it" in her mother, "it" in your wife may use sex to reduce your male authority and so produce that weak or violent father she enjoyed hating.

You see, "it" thrives on cruel pressure and also enjoys feeding "its" contempt on your resentment-born weakness. This is why you must be strong and patient, and with long-suffering, bear the tribulations "it" will inflict upon you. Be strengthened by the knowledge that "it" is only pulling your beloved's strings. Your beloved is not evil—"it" is. The evil "it" wants you to be impatient, weak, resentful, even violent—then "it" is justified and renewed in you. Always remember that your real wife or child needs the strength that emanates through patience; their real will has been smothered. They cannot tell you what their real needs are, but I can.

They want you to STOP "it" in them, but with patience and love—with a FORCE—a NON-VIOLENT FORCE.

Good is a FORCE.

Evil is a FORCE, *but evil fears the force of good;* therefore, "it" inside you will trick you into doubting the use of force.

Evil can force you to reject the education, the religion, even the very Truth which can save you. "It" does this by *impatiently* forcing everything down your throat, for "your own good." But Good never pushes anything down anyone's throat.

I know how tempting it is to bust some mocking person in the mouth, to knock the hell out of them and teach them a lesson. I know that when you are tempted to resent, "it" has tricked you into reinforcing "its" errant behavior. You might easily beat someone into the ground for not seeing something your way, but what good does this do? As a bully-parent, you develop a weak, frightened child—or one who grows up out-bullying you.

Perhaps you are afraid of being strong because you fear what you might do. Then again, perhaps you don't want to be hated by your child (the way you hated your parents) and that makes you too soft with him or her. That is the very weakness which feeds contempt and conceit in your child—or anyone.

Although what you try to accomplish may be right in the letter, the spirit of it becomes ineffective because it is weak and tainted by impatience and resentment. You are guilty now for being too weak or too strong. Perhaps this is why you associate this guilt feeling with the good you were trying to impose, and that makes you think you are wrong about the *principle*. That could compel you to back off. You try to keep the peace to avoid violence; you suppress your resentment. You are soft, silent when you should speak up and act. In selfishness, your pride is more concerned with its own ease and peace, with staying calm (not guilty) rather than with doing right—which you can't anyway.

So we have the force of Hell and the consent of Hell.

Hell's silence is the kind of silence that stands mute, feeding and supporting the beast in your charges. It is the kind of permissive silence on which Hell's own nature in your child feeds. In your violent silence, you indulge in judging everything that is going wrong with your family. In this kind of silence, one is so busy creating or permitting wrong that one never sees one's own wrong. Silence is often cowardice calculated to feed the judgment value of another's wickedness. So for a while there is no violence, only an eerie peace, while you appease another in the process of developing his "monster."

Both good and evil have their own silence and their own force, you see.

When we are wrong and when, in our pride, we have lost the power to change things for the good, the only good we know is the kind that promotes and then compares itself with the bad in others. We have cultivated those very evils because of love's original failing. We are in agreement when we stand in silent consent and, again, when we enjoy our judgment.

I said you are afraid of being forceful because you don't want to make trouble, or perhaps you don't want to be like the parent you hated. The guilt formed by fear and violence in you makes you need love. This need for "love" is really something gone wrong in you, seeking support by being weak. In your wrong (seeking approval) you support the wrong of another for approval. That really is a selfish love, a devilish concern for another (devil). And every spoiled brat loves/hates that in you—and promptly grows meaner. You will give in to demands until you have a nervous breakdown, fueled by resentment.

The violence in you (from your parents) may seek "peace," but, frankly, it can't stand true peace very long because it needs intrigue more. You can only find that restless peace as an appeaser (one who never speaks up or opposes evil). For that kind of peace, you must give more and more of your self, more and more ground, until sooner or later you find yourself chained to the very hate and violence you fear—and strangely need.

Your children, from whom you need love, and your wife, whom you selfishly appease, become the enemies whom you must one day fight if you are to survive. To survive, you must become more violent than they are. Dreading that violence and fearing that you will become like them forces you to grub in the dirt, to shrink into a shell, to experience this seething "quiet" until the dam bursts, turning all that pent-up violence outward onto them, or inward, onto yourself. Is it not remarkable that after thousands of years of studying human nature, no one (but One) has pointed out the need for patience in dealing with others? The emotions of pride (resentment in particular) cause all our problems.

Every person who needs correction is sinking in the struggle with this love-hate thing, rebelling and conforming to impatient authorities.

110

Some people are very easy to correct; which is to say, they respond very quickly to admonishment, but the change is superficial. Here you may find yourself obliged to go on patiently correcting them until you lose your patience. You see, as long as the spirit of the person is wrong, there will be this eagerness to please the wrong nature in you. Any change of behavior is calculated, a conditioned failure which the victim quickly converts to an asset by gaining approval for it. He agrees with you to escape the Spirit of Truth. He literally trains a spirit of violence and hypocrisy in you to serve his "thing."

There is no meaningful change here. You are always secretly resented for being a dictator, and a dictator is what people need to serve (love), or defy (hate). So you can find yourself being placed in the position of a hated authority figure. You find yourself becoming irritated for the growing responsibility to correct everyone. Watch out for this sort of thing and, through well-timed conversation, point out the game being played.

The rebel spouse or child must be handled differently. While the conformist submits, placing you in the hated-but-needed pressure/authority role and *secretly* enjoying hating you, the rebel openly enjoys making you push him. He will act just the opposite from your wishes to tempt you to push. His entire rebellion act is fueled by reacting (resentment) against *your will*. This kind of "it" evolves from contest, while the conformist's "it" evolves from submission. Now, if you are not willful, they both lose the steam they need to grow; they begin to lose the sustaining force for their pride. Their pride of conforming or their pride of rebelling comes from *your* pride of dominating.

As I have said before, man was created to respond to his own enlightened reason. If you can dissolve your pride and let that happen, you help your child discover the response to his own logic rather than to your will; then all the problems between you vanish. Your willful, prideful, pushy, ambitious, selfish authority is the basis for his weakness and/or rebellion. When that ceases in you, it also ceases in your children. Soon all is well.

Suppose, for instance, I told you not to smoke. Would I not be applying pressure, getting a reaction which tears you further away from being able to respond to yourself? Surely that very reaction is what is causing conflict and tension which, in turn, needs to be soothed by something—smoke, drink, food, drugs—the very thing I'm telling you to give up.

Now I see you becoming a drunk, an addict, a fatso, and that upsets me. My upset upsets you. I scream, holler, rant and rave (for your own "good," of course), but that only makes you rebel against your own best interest. You want so badly to be your own person that you smoke when I tell you not to. While you are smoking, you may think it is dumb, but you do it anyway, trying to be "free" by being the opposite of what my will wants. While I can get "high" nagging you not to smoke or drink, you can get high smoking and drinking (or doing whatever is forbidden). And, believe it or not, nagging is the way any nagger keeps himself/herself from drinking, smoking, being a cannibal or whatever. He regiments himself by promoting in someone else the very weakness from which he is escaping.

Your kids can no more help rebelling than you can stop yourself from pressuring them or trying to "save" them.

But don't be surprised if you end up doing those dumb things yourself. The logic is that when you become upset at failing to help them (and how they enjoy defeating your will!), the tension in you creates a need for the same pleasures you tried to protect them from. Since you can't lick 'em, you join 'em. You see, you feel guilty for trying and failing. In the struggle, you become as sick as they are. You become as rotten as they are to avoid criticism, to gain acceptance from the "bums" you've created.

Now you are overeating, drinking, smoking, to ease the pain of guilt and conflict; you are like what you started out loving and ended up hating. The pride in you has projected what *you are*, and evolved the pride and the problem in others. For a while, looking at that distracts you from seeing your own indwelling evil. Hating them, being sorry for them, trying to help them, all are part of the same sickness. This sickness has to do with having been corrupted when you were young. The spirit of good and love that might have lived within you, was set aside by the *prideful spirit of impatience,* which is still projecting and taking a number of different forms in you and your family.

This ambitious spirit living in you breeds guilt, a sense of inferiority and failure which drives you to remedy the problem by the way you live through your offspring. When the familiar conforming and rebelling occurs, that spirit feels a sense of *elation,* of growth, of achievement in the struggle. On one hand, you can swell up with pride when your child shows you in a good light; on the other hand, when his rebellion threatens and challenges, you can try harder to "improve" him by destroying his individuality.

You may want the best for your children, but it is always

accomplished in an ungodly way. The kind of character that develops out of constant pressure is not one which serves God, but serves the spirit behind corruption. This is why the successful man or woman is never happy with success: because of what he/she becomes in the process of succeeding. One can even *fear* success for this reason.

The rebel exists to provide *every* conformist with a sense of worth. Comparing himself to those low-life rebels, a conformist might become a judge, a social worker, policeman, doctor, lawyer, preacher, whatever "helps" (or punishes) the rebels *which these kinds have created.* The hypocrite perpetuates all the evils of his mentors, driving mankind to crime, sickness, insanity on one hand—curing, reforming and punishing him on the other.

Find, therefore, the spirit of patience: *the non-violent force.* No need to fear using force here because you know that without the back-up of force you are impotent. It has been employment of *the wrong kind of force* (impatience) which reinforced the problem in others, the guilt and fear of force in yourself. Your wife and children really need that strength, that strong stand, that contrast, to awaken them to the error of their ways. Sometimes they *have to be* stopped because the suggestions of friends in them are so powerful that nothing short of physical intervention will do.

They need you to stop them.

They will hate you if you let them go, if you are too soft and weak. If you need their love, if you are fearful of hurting them by binding them or afraid of your own violence, then you are impotent. A strong "no" with courage of conviction, backed up if need be with non-angry, non-violent *force* is often the answer. And as children grow older, they will see the truth whenever they resent your loving authority; they will quickly become ashamed and tell you they are sorry. Do not make the fatal error of reasoning with them endlessly. It will take reasonable *force* to overturn the unreasoning force within them.

Correction based on resentment blocks positive change. Resentment *tempts* them to hate and reject and evolve that pride they see in you. It justifies and fuels the compulsion to do wrong or to be a hypocritical, people-pleasing destroyer of the next generation.

In order to correct your wife and children, it is absolutely necessary to separate them from the hypnotic, supportive influence of their friends. If you do not have the love, *the force* to tear them away from that world, you will fail to save them from themselves and you too will suffer from this failing.

Each time a woman loves a man in the special way that supports his ego, that man's soul will find itself at war with God—in other words, in conflict with himself. His ego may like the feeling of support so much that he will serve the female manipulator more and more, becoming less and less able to be responsive to what is right and wise. Try to tell this to a man who is in love and he will resent you and cling to the supportive female love. This is also true of children with their friends, music and other vices.

A person reacts to correction by a friend or father exactly the way he responds to his own conscience. The Bible tells us that the love (support) of the world is enmity with God. So everything which pleases—supporting the ego life and causing us to cling to and pursue it, to do its will for the sake of that support—makes us resent those who disturb us from our sleep in pleasure.

By now you should be able to see more clearly what your own problem is and the forces that you face in your children. The undue love and admiration of strangers has more power than ordinary parental love or goodness. The support from their "friends" casts a spell which must be broken at its source by an opposing force. Therefore, you must determine, without malice or anger, to separate your children from their (wrong) friends and keep constant vigilance so that things do not become too cozy again.

Be careful that your own vices and needs for phony ego-supporting friends do not justify your children's needs to have their own. Here again, your own failing will tempt them to have their own brand of sin. *You must have no vices.* You cannot admonish anyone against anything with drink or cigarette in hand. The absence of virtue is SIN and those who sleep in sin cannot awaken others from the false security of sin.

On the other hand, once you are sincerely committed, then you have power and wisdom. The love and authority which do not tempt are then fully able to redeem. With solemn and unyielding conviction, separate your wife and child from the sustaining hypnosis of friends. *If you fail here, you will fail all the way down the line.* They are not strong enough to do this for themselves. They owe allegiance to others by virtue of an ego need which they don't understand and which they think is good. They are fascinated by the affection of the world that is corrupting and addicting them to pleasures and they like it so much that they cannot tear themselves away even though they (may) know it is killing them. Secretly, deep down inside, *they want you to say "NO!"* Because of the commotion and fight they put up, you may not believe that is so, but wait a little while and see what happens in time.

You must say "no" then, without anger or resentment, with non-violent force. A woman knows that touch, a child knows that feeling; even the newborn can experience it and feel secure.

You don't have to go to school to be mature, to recognize the difference between the touch of violence and the touch of love. Grab someone with violence and you immediately reinforce the evil within them, while you yourself are in danger of being injected by their evil and their violence. But grab hold of someone because you care enough to be physical with them, and you introduce something new: the salvation of love. Your love-force gets inside and goes to war with the bad spirit; soon the battle is won and they feel better, even grateful.

But when you "correct" your children with resentment, then resentment only reinforces what is wrong in the child. The wrong—your wrong—gets in, but correction stays out. The same kind of thing often occurs with students. They may be eager to learn at first, but an impatient teacher can easily ruin all of that. The student reacts defensively to the hostility of the teacher, which keeps knowledge out and lets errant behavior in.

The "authority" in most cases is responsible for making kids worse while apparently trying to make them better. If power and authority were your secret motive, you would never be out of work, simply because you would be *creating* problems to solve by means of the very process of "solving" them.

So it is very important to be patient when attempting to correct other people. You must be forceful enough to drive the point home, but without resentment. The force I speak of is love, a deep, abiding caring, backed by the absolute certainty of the good you are doing and the knowledge of what is right. Remember, you can't be like that when *you* are upset and angry too! Meditate on this fact before you go to war with the error in others.

You must be absolutely willing to go as far as you must go, never backing down once you start. If your children are smoking dope and listening to too much hard rock, then for their sakes you must put your foot down and separate them from these hypnotic influences. You must be strong and sure. You must be ready to take a lot of complaints and cursing. You must be ready to lose their love and friendship—to be alone, if that's what it takes. Your children are not strong enough to separate themselves from their habits and friends. You must do that for them. That is what love is all about. They literally cannot free themselves from the spell of the world. They really want you to say, "No, you cannot go out with so-and-so," and "No, you can't have your record player until you learn to be more responsible, not caught up with these things."

The rule in my house is that if my kids can't influence their friends for the good, they can't have friends— because what kind of friends would they then be? They must lead others toward the good life and never follow the bad. What child could really argue with that?

Let the Truth, firmly spoken, do its work. You must not put effort or energy behind it. You will know that you are doing it right when you don't have frustration and don't feel guilty afterward.

I am not saying that your correction will "take" immediately; it may not *ever*. You will never be free in yourself until you give your child or spouse the kind of opportunity they need. When you stand for what is right, you give others an opportunity to change which they never had before in their lives. If they reject that, it's their problem, not yours.

Let us say you are making them worse through some secret hostility. That hostility, because it is there inside you, will make you feel guilt. That guilt and your failure to correct them may threaten your ego and make you try harder. Perhaps their rebellion will feed the hostility in you and make you try even harder to correct them, always with an adverse effect on you and a reverse effect on your victim. You are locked in a prison together.

When you stand as a loving correction, a different energy is engaged. Love gets through the old defenses. It has the effect of awakening your child to see that you are right in what you say and in what you are. It speaks love instead of hate, so he can accept that correction of love.

The problem in this world lies with wrong authority. People are hurt by all kinds of wrong authorities. However, it is good for them to recognize and respond to a *good* authority because it reverses the effect of responding to the *bad* one.

I remember people giving me good advice which I never took in my early years. Looking back, I realize that if those people who gave those words of advice had spoken with love, it would have jolted me to realize what I needed to realize then. I would not have made so many errors.

Fathers, especially, are often too weak with the Truth they speak. The reason for this is that they lack love. They are more interested in preserving comfortable relationships; they selfishly want to *get* love. So they may speak Truth; they may admonish and give good advice, but they are ineffective because they want to be popular.

They don't want to hurt anyone's feelings. No one can blame *them*. After all, they did tell you, didn't they? They tried to stop you, didn't they?

Sick people may not mind your speaking the Truth, as long as you are not effective, as long as the Truth is weak and their ego is stronger. They will "love" you for your weak speeches because your attempts to help them actually strengthen the error inside them.

Be like a general who, before he goes to war, takes an accounting of all the weapons he has. If he is not more powerful than his enemy and cannot win, he will lose everything to the enemy.

True confidence in what you know is best for your child is your arsenal of strength. Realize what a hornet's nest you are getting into before you start—or your life won't be worth a plug nickel.

8: What Kind of Woman Marries a Wimp?

A woman has to be more careful than a man about choosing a mate. Especially, she should watch out for "Mr. Nice," the super-obliging Cheshire cat. No matter how honest and hardworking, or how "devoted" a husband to her such a man may be, if she learns he is not devoted first to justice, to an unmistakable divine fire within, she will eat him alive. A woman deeply desires to respect her husband, so much so that the frustration of living with a sweet but characterless animal can bring out the witch in her and drive her to drink and to other men. Unfortunately, most women are drawn to weak men—to "Mr. Meek and Mild, the Friendly Fiend."

Let's delve into the mystery of this weak and passive "woman's man."

Good, in its purest sense, is what every woman—like it or not—needs. Fair and Firm is the only authority over guile. By patiently jousting with her spirit, the husband possessed of such authority can rescue his wife from the agony of pride. But agreeable Mr. Nice, by virtue of his guileful support (a sort of false love), serves instead only to frustrate and corrupt her.

Perhaps you see the same kind of invisible genie forces corrupting your children, acting through their supportive friends. You may see the danger of such friendships, but your children cannot; it is natural for their budding egos to enjoy being stroked. Their thinking is, "What can be so bad about what makes me feel good?"

No mind involved in pleasure can be possessed of objectivity or foresight. It's up to you to do something to protect your children. But by standing *angrily* between them and their various craven needs (wants), you make matters worse. Your emotional interference reverses your intent, energizing their determination in favor of foolish endeavors and associations. Yet, if you stand silent, your seeming assent supports their faults in another way. What you do and fail to do will both make matters worse—and this principle holds true for just about any human situation imaginable.

Likelier than not, if you have a problem, its cause was a milquetoast or violent father. A weak dad sets one up to choose or to become a weak husband. Being a weak man means that you have a lot more of your mother in you than you perhaps care to see, and it is her nature in you that is attracted to the same kind of female spirit (dominant-supportive) in a wife. Conversely, female offspring of a dominant mother and passive father are attracted to men they can mold and rule (or save)—for exactly the same ego reasons the mother had for marrying a weak man.

As you read on, bear in mind a theme that will recur throughout this text: Dominant and supportive women are one and the same, and weak and violent men are one and the same. These apparent opposites attract and evolve evil between them.

In other words, if a man who hates his vile mother thinks to escape her by marrying a sweet, supportive woman, he has it all wrong. Submissive people-pleasers are seeking the opportunity to dominate. Conquest through submission is a sneaky strategy of the weak, and marriages that begin with female submission end with female dominance. One morning the deluded male is rudely awakened to the presence in his bed of either a vicious tyrant, or a hypocritical, "sweet" subtle manipulator.

The woman, on her part, "chooses" a man who excites her because he is malleable clay. Just as every spoiled brat "loves" those who let him have his way, a woman who was unloved (uncorrected) by a father will attract and favor weak men. But she will never be comfortable with the control she thus acquires. Sure, she may get everything she "wants"—all the material things, but never what she needs and *truly* wants: correction from having been spoiled. She has chosen a hopeless, romantic, female-worshiper, who in exchange for her approval lets her make all the decisions, and gives her everything she demands, because approval is all he lives for. Also (another benefit), he gets to judge her for everything that goes wrong. The game of pride is to win.

Mr. Nice is never wrong in his own eyes. If he "lets" you be the boss, it's only because he is a born loser anyway. Too gutless to win respect by asserting himself, he gives in to you to get support for his failing and to convert failing into virtue. When things go wrong, he gets another ego boost by sitting on his perch, puffed up with pride, smiling in delirious judgment.

Every Mr. Nice is really a submissive woman inside,

the wretched product of an unmanly (or absent) father and an uncorrected mother. This kind of man uses female ways to retrieve the command of his lost manhood. What typically emerges, of course, is a more submissive woman in a man's body. How can he become a real man using sly, seductive methods: surrendering in order to take charge? Will he not either strengthen his wife's role of powerful tyrant, or at best become that power—become a tyrant himself?

In the realm of the ego, being "right" is equal in value to being powerful. So even though Mr. Nice's violent wife may remain as she is, a mean, masculine, animal power in the home, Mr. Nice can see himself as hard done by; he is "Mr. Right," by comparison with her, and is thus her equal or superior. We see here the reverse of a common male-female relationship: The woman's efforts to seduce the man out of his (beastly) power succeed only in feeding his violence; but she has her consolation in seeing herself as the martyred "Mrs. Right."

When the authority of grace is lost, a lower, compensatory form of authority can appear—the authority of a jungle hell. Here again we see the classic symptom of submission at work, its desperate effort to subdue the violence that originally it caused. The cowering, frightened (guileful) female, finding she cannot make the beast she has aroused serve her cause, makes use of its evolving wickedness by comparing it with her goodness. You know the type. She is like a weak president who sees himself as a peace-maker, who in fact is only appeasing and supporting evil, thus encouraging greater evil to appear—as war.

The smug hypocrisy of this type of woman promotes

the evil that she needs to see in a man in order to feel the "security" of being superior to it. A selfish ego that cannot win power through seduction must settle for the satisfaction of judgment—the sense of self-righteousness that the slave of a vicious master enjoys. For many, the only way to glory is through the role of a tortured, brutalized slave. If a woman's ego cannot use a man one way, it will use him in another. Believe me when I say, *"weakness is the handmaiden of wickedness."*

Are you a frustrated, angry woman living with seductive Mr. Right? Then you know what it is like to live in a man's shoes, which hopefully will awaken in you a modicum of compassion for your poor victim. That through our sins we change roles may be God's way of helping us understand the sufferings of others. Judgment of and seething contempt for your parents can infect you with your parents' nature. Watch out for evidence of this in your conduct with your children.

To have a man cater to her every whim makes a woman feel so good, that it can be convenient for her to believe she is in love with this Mr Nice. Perhaps you used an available Mr. Nice to escape from an intolerable home life. If so, you have plenty of company. Perhaps you lost yourself in a Mr. Nice to escape the guilt and inferiority you felt because of hatred for a "Mr. Violent"—your father. Oh, yes, deep down you may have really wanted a good man, but you were so fearful of being dominated (even by a good man) that you were overwhelmed and taken in by "Mr. Meek and Mild." While you were cowering before your mean father and hating him, you were becoming like him inside. This is something that is hard to face, but you will see it revealed in a relationship with anyone weaker than yourself—with a weak husband or your children.

When a chance to dominate presents itself, we feel alive and powerful, important, brave and secure. Given someone weaker to dominate, we feel relief—the same relief our parents felt in ruling us after a lifetime of being ruled themselves. Alas, these "good" feelings of security are at the expense of others; our happiness rests on the destruction of theirs, on degrading them and making them sacrifice and suffer. It is all a deception based on the ego principle of comparison and relativity. From a basic madness a greater madness is always evolving and manifesting. The enemy you hate and fear and would flee is actually becoming you inside you!

Alas, the truly guileful are rarely awakened by suffering as the sincere person is. I am trying to say that if you can accept these hard truths, the chances are that you have been but a victim of the cycle (evil evolving evil), and therefore may hope for salvation. For what child could emerge unscathed from the traumas of family violence?

What a dilemma! You run from Mr. Mean to Mr. Nice; then, to escape the hell of power raised in you through living with a weakling, you run screaming from Mr. Nice to Mr. Mean, only to find yourself living as a weakling with the "father" you hated as a child!

The female guile is everywhere, perverting all relationships. A woman with a man inside her can be sexually attracted to a man with a woman inside him. Her maleness can make her feel as though she is married to her own mother; or to his (his mother being similar to her own). What I am saying is that the confusing female spirit intruding where it does not belong fouls up all healthy life and love relationships.

When we pull away the disguise, we see Mr. Nice revealed as a female spirit occupying a male body. So long as you intoxicate yourself with the image Mr. Nice projects, you will not be aware of the exchange between you that is taking place. It can be an incredible cunning devil indeed. The rule of thumb is: submission induces violence when it fails of its object, which is to ascend to power to become violent itself.

No one can escape the spirit of guile that stalks the earth since man's fall from grace. Violent men attract submissive women, women who are conditioned to the role of mothering and spoiling violent men. And submissive men attract violent women. Everywhere there is intrigue. Nowhere is the spirit of grace to be found.

Were a businessman firm and fair with his employees, there would be no need for a union. But because he is otherwise, a union evolves, and because of its likeness to the corrupt management, it eventually destroys the company. In the same way, graceless politics evolve suspicion, rivalry and violence between countries. There can be no peace until there is grace.

So it is in all human affairs. When grace prevails, evil ceases to evolve, and there are no losers—only winners.

Now a generation of vipers has emerged—womanly men and manly women seeking from each other their lost roles and powers. Like his weak father before him, who gave his wife power, Mr. Nice feels most secure (powerful or right) in the presence of a strong, dominating woman. To him weakness is not surrender, but a strategy of the ego for survival and conquest, learned from his role-exchanged parents. He may see himself as magnificently loyal, loving, benevolent and worthy, when really he is a cat patiently waiting for the master to leave so he can pounce on his dinner.

Poor woman, no wonder you are confused! You cannot understand your craving for the kind of man who inspires in you only judgment and contempt. The bully who has contempt for the coward needs the coward to feel secure, because bully is all he knows. But what does that contempt do? Does it awaken the cowardly lion? No, it only frightens him into a more contemptible cowardice, making the bully meaner.

When grace fails in a man, in that void left where grace no longer is, an evil (which could not otherwise be) manifests in the form of Mr. Mean and masquerades as a Mr. Nice. No matter how these two behave, they turn the wheel of chaos and confusion, of the slave-tyrant relationships that have established on this planet the rule of evil and the Fall.

Can you see why Mr. Nice is no damn good, and why what you have thought of as good—your good, his good, anyone's good—is nothing but a selfish game of pride? Nice is not necessarily the opposite of mean; your false "good" introduces and reinforces "mean," and mean reinforces phony good. Such goodness is just another form of wickedness; it is the weakness that we have called "the handmaiden of evil."

So, if you are one of those Mr. Meek and Mild weaklings, expect to have a wild, frustrated wife. And if you are scratching your wooden head wondering what it is she wants from your animal carcass, ask yourself, while you are about it, just why are you so nice? Are you not pleasing her in order to get her devil to grant you a sense of worth, to help you deny to yourself what you are—a fallen, miserable, selfish, wretched creep?

Sure, you crave "love" from her, but only because you have yourself withheld, preferring to use her, the true love you might have given her. What she thinks of you has been more important to you than standing up for what is right, and the little good you have left in you, you are willing to sacrifice for that brownie button of her approval. Like the first man, Adam, you don't correct your wife because your ego *needs* the hell in her. To serve you. To reinforce your pride and ambition. To make you feel like a man when you are not.

Your misguided mother had little tolerance for your dad's natural authority. With the power he gave up to her, her impatient, hungry spirit saw to it that male children knuckled under, thus implanting in them a nature that could survive only in relationships with dominating females. Now you, a corrupted, womanizing man, have little concern for what is right. You enjoy being violated—and violating, with seduction and violence. Gladly and pridefully you sacrifice true worth for *feelings* of worth that women give you. You carefully cultivate and preserve a sick relationship by never "offending" the lady, while in fact doing her mortal harm with your loveless giving in and walking around on eggshells. (Politically speaking, liberals are like this. They are like guileful women, seeking power by cultivating the worst in society for the sake of gaining power.)

You can give a woman the true love she needs only by giving up the ego feelings of worth that you crave from her reassurances. She may have become afraid to reassure you by serving your wants, because of what this

129

does to you both. She cannot stand for you to touch her, because of what that touch draws up in her and in you. She has seen you become a weakling or beast, and herself become a coward or beast, until—if she has any honesty left—all she can do is strike out at you like a cornered animal, or scream out her contempt (hopefully with a cry to God to save her from such judgment of you)—which scares you into buying her flowers!

You have become an animal and, as such, you need affection for the beast you have become. You need to be stroked like a Cheshire cat, to be comforted by your master-corruptor. You womanize and people-please for such comfort, and the gratifying of your ever growing need to be stroked, you confuse with love and goodness.

From time immemorial, a woman's body has been used (idolized) in witchcraft rituals as a means of calling up the devil. Is it any wonder, sir, that your life is a living hell? What you need is grace, the kind of inward wholesomeness that does not need the reassurances of others' love and approval. Do you see how your selfish need and weakness make you part of the system? Without grace you cannot separate from it, you must evolve like an animal and submit to the animal.

Let me address myself to a Mr. Nice who has divorced and remarried, determined to try harder this time to make the marriage work. Stop for a moment and consider the pressure you feel not to repeat past mistakes, to bend over backwards to please by being more "kind" and condescending than ever. See how your pride is still involved, struggling to make up for failure with one woman through more failure with another, instead of asking God for salvation through His grace. You have not yet learned your lesson.

Sensing your desperation to make things work, your new (and, more often than not, sicker) wife takes every liberty she can, twisting you around her little finger, making your life a double-hell. Because trying to make things work is the work of will, it can be frustrated by other wills. Whereas if you had no will but the Heavenly Father's, you could not be frustrated. You see, His will is there when yours is not. It is simple as that. You need a gracious but don't-give-a-damn-what-she-thinks-of-me outlook. Your new wife and family are expendable, in the sense that your problem can only work out if you *stop caring too much what they think of you.* You must stop trying to force this marriage to "work" (selfishly for you). You need not make up for past failings with others. The pride of life blinds and distorts facts; it can cause you to misinterpret the meaning of guilt and to think your past mistakes were caused by your not being "good" enough. Pride will not let you see your false goodness (people-pleasing) as weakness, so instead of realizing and finding grace, you become "nicer" than ever.

You need humility to experience true love. You need *to* love, to care for, rather than to *be* loved and cared for. *Through patience possess ye your soul.*

A real Mr. Right is not out to win a popularity contest, nor is he so egotistical as to think he can make up for anything. Admitting wrong and not seeking support wins the approval of the Father. Therefore, there is no need to care a tinker's cuss what anyone thinks, as long as you know your course is just. With such an attitude, you will be able to perceive reality, to determine what is fair and unfair. You will not concede to pressure, no matter the loss or gain. This is the manliness that evokes the respect of the real women. Suddenly grace appears and disgrace disappears.

There are two forces working inside you. One loves the Truth, and the other does not—because the Truth threatens its needs. Selfishness may claim to love the Truth, for appearances' sake may "agree" with it, or even go so far as to preach it; but in practice it never gives up the fun and adventure of the egotistical life. And that is why intrigue flourishes.

For standing on principle, you may well lose the ego-support of the approval of friends, or even of sex privileges with your wife. Suffer such rejection, and in trembling receive grace. Fearful of losing worldly benefits, no Mr. Nice can come shining through, simply because a selfishness-beast is all there is of him. His entire existence depends on cultivating the wrong in the woman in order to use it. Therefore recognize your need is not true love. Neutralize that need for acceptance, and be not troubled nor resentful in the face of rejection. Only the real man can successfully undergo this trial. If you will, be that man, and in time, to your astonishment, you will discover you have gained your family's love and respect; because that quality appearing in you through your trial is what every woman and child is really seeking in a husband and father. Once grace exists within you, evil cannot.

The vanity of a female seeks to possess what it cannot. She wants, loves, admires and respects the man she can never "have"—if you see what I mean. If you give in to her subtle pressures and she "gets" you, she cannot then feel respect for you, and a woman *needs* to respect her husband. Unfulfilled in this need, insecure with you and discontented, all that remains for her is the revenge of getting to you, making you suffer in payment for your failure to be a true husband—one who would stop her with love.

Men and women are free to do good only to the degree that they are free from the need for approval. Through caring too much, you tempt your children to take advantage of your "good" nature and are therefore powerless to stop them from going astray.

Caring too much means caring only for yourself. Such caring is not caring at all except for Number One. The man who really cares for his family, who is *concerned* for them, is less emotionally involved with them, so that he may stand firm on all principle, patiently, come what may. No one really respects the weak and the selfish. They are "admired" only to be used. Dare you speak up or stand as a correction to anyone whose favor you selfishly need? Of course not! All selfish people are bound to lose their freedom of speech, and eventually all their freedoms.

More often than not, we have an ulterior motive for being nice; our object is to manipulate, whether to get the mechanic to fix our car properly or to get someone to give us a job—whatever. But people aren't always fooled. The more sophisticated see through such niceness to the weakness behind it, which tempts them to take the advantage you are seeking from them.

When I said your family is expendable, it was to help you realize that salvation does not depend upon your bringing anyone around. In any situation, merely patiently hold fast—through all the kicking, cursing, pressuring and fussing—to what is clearly wise, fair, sensible and just. The salvation of your children and family depend on two things: 1) your standing firm on principle, making principle unmistakably clear; and 2) their choosing to stand with you on the side of principle, it having been made clear to them. The choice must be theirs alone, for God wants volunteers, not conscripts. That is why you must get your own will in the matter out of the way.

Remember that your family are moral beings with moral choices. You rob them of their chance to *choose* the right when, in your own desperation, you pressure, manipulate, oblige or in some way try to force them to be right. By such means you make them either rebel against you, or capitulate to you in meek surrender. What point is there in sweet-talking or forcing them into being good? If you do this, it is certainly not because you care for them, rather it is because you think by "saving" them you save yourself, or because your ego cannot bear another failure, or because you simply enjoy power. Such an attitude will make any marriage fail. Your family can see when your caring for them to be right is not for their sakes but for its reflection on you. It is desperation on your own account that changes you from a Mr. Nice into a Mr. Mean, trying to knock some sense into your family. I'm not saying that force should not be used at times—to keep your kids from going with bad company, for instance—but it must be a force in which they recognize love—a true, fatherly caring for them.

Do you see now what I mean by expendable? If through pure intent you reveal what true caring for them is and your family responds favorably, their choosing right is good for them and naturally pleasing to you. But if they reject the persistent good you show them, too bad for them! They will have had their chance at life through you and you will have had your second chance. Their choosing wrong *should not faze you one little bit.* It has become their problem, not yours. You can rest assured that you did what was right. Do you see why it is not up to you to save anyone? Why you are responsible only for showing the way? Your role is to stand as a contrast, not a temptation.

You cannot know how God is working to fulfill His purpose for you. He may have given you a second family to teach you a lesson and to work out a happy ending for all. On the other hand, you may find your second family more incorrigible than the first. You may show wisdom and strength you did not have with your first family, yet still not get the response *you* egotistically want. That this family cannot appreciate your goodness may be another test for you. Your wife may have a wicked harlot's heart. Knowing how egotistically desperate you are, she is pleased to frustrate your reaching your goal every which way she can, all the way to hell and dragging you with her. So there must be no will, no goal. There must be only patience and long-suffering, and never mind the outcome.

Understanding the Truth, you may bring joy to a potentially good family, or frustration to a wicked one. Either way, walk tall; feel gladness; smile.

9: The Manly Woman

The mother who has corrupted her husband has two natures: some of his and some of her own, and she becomes the custodian of those natures for her children. She is obliged to rise as a strong mother to meet her husband's need for a mother, but grows to become as a father with a child. The woman becomes the man and the man becomes the woman—everything is back to front.

Woman was so called because she *came out* of man. Woman was originally man's child and man was destined to become like a father. Since the original corruption, man has come out of woman and, being born of her, is mysteriously subject to her authority. Woman, with a little too much man in her, and man, with a little too much woman in him, are male and female, respectively. Once the male authority is transferred permanently to the woman through man's default (original sin), sin goes on eating out the male substance. When the process is completed, the male-female roles are completely reversed.

Happily, the enlightened, strong, faithful father is custodian of his child's real identity. In him resides the authority to cause his sons to identify with him (and his

Creator) and to inspire the female child to seek his high standard of moral strength in her mate. Unfortunately, just the reverse occurs when the female evolves to become the head of the family. In her ignorance, she deals out to the male child a female identity and, conversely, projects into the female child the authority of her own adopted male nature. The male identity in the daughter now grows up to become the strong mother that other female-centered boys (hoping to escape their despotic mothers) seek out in their wives. Again, you have that strong-mother/weak-father syndrome producing sets of mother-centered children.

Every female power trip carries with it a built-in diminishing return. At various moments, the mother-in-the-wife is struck with the terrifying realization that she is losing her femininity through a bizarre exchange inherent in all temptations, which then transforms into the inherited prideful will to power. Never having known true love, the ego power trip is the only security she has, but being denied this false security, she feels alone, guilty and insecure. Her choice now is between the devil and the deep blue sea: more clammy security derived from male sexual failing, or that terrible void caused by guilt. Almost every woman knows that sexual politics lead back to the knowledge of the abyss that exists without them. She needs what she loathes.

Guilt always arises from observing herself playing the sick role of mother-of-the-beast. Unfortunately, the prideful spirit within her twists this observation around to its own advantage, making her think that the guilt is evidence that she is not "enough woman" for her man. Thus misguided, she is driven and encouraged by her stupid mate. She repeats the same terrible mistake. Alas, instead of becoming more of a woman through the traditional give-love-to-get-love tease, she becomes more masculine, the personification of some kind of a demon. Now she is terrified.

Next, the unholy spirit goes on to teach her how to maintain her femininity and yet hold fast to the false security which power gives her. You see, ordinary fallen males have no power unless, of course, they are completely female inside. Therefore, if she is to hold on to "security," she must somehow hold on to that elusive femininity. To accomplish this goal, the tormented female takes to cruelly teasing her daughter.

Some females want to give birth to boys (to feed on) while others look forward to having little girls. One of the secret motives for wanting female offspring is to provide a body to which she can transfer her excess masculine essence which clings from power con games played with husbands and boyfriends. That, in a nutshell, is why young girls find themselves becoming aggressive like their mothers: they learn that an aggressive male nature in a woman is what attracts, excites and reassures the female nature in a weak, failing man.

A masculine mother can also use her daughter as if she were a son or husband, pushing her to achieve, the way wives pressure their menfolk. Through the child's response to her pressure-tease, mother again exchanges natures with her daughter, thereby holding onto an external semblance of femininity and remaining exciting to men. It's like having her cake and eating it too, because this way she can go on playing the power game with a dying mate, whore around with other "men," then come home and unload the sin, the essence and guilt *into* her daughter while stealing the child's innocence, femininity, health—even her youth.

Because of her falling to mother's guile, the child carries the heavy burden of her mother's sin. She must secretly cope with that male feeling and burning as best she can. But how? Usually it is in the classic way: hoping to be more woman by pleasing more men—lots of sex and tease. Even if it is not her intention, she goes through the same old ritual as a guileful witch playing the power game, becoming uglier and more masculine. Like it or not, she becomes like her sergeant-major or whorish mother. God help the beasts and little children!

Through unspeakable cruelty, the victim can become old before her time. Mother can remain relatively youthful and healthy while the daughter inherits her mother's guileful, even criminal nature, plus the complexity and conflict of her *male* nature. In the eyes of the world, the child appears to have the problem rather than the wicked mother or the weak father. Usually the child is aware that it is the parent who is sick, but that knowledge itself doesn't help; it only serves as a torment. The emotional upset again reinforces the mother-identity in the child, which is tantamount to a "cure" for the mother. Generally speaking, unloading sin is the way all the damned "free" themselves of guilt—temporarily.

Let us suppose for a moment that the child recovers her self and calmly resists the sick mother's pressures. A strange thing happens: mother starts going mad, and threatened by her daughter's innocence, she tries harder to confuse, to make her daughter feel guilty for her sins once again. Mother may go to the extreme tease: being nice and being mean alternately, trying to confound her victim. She may make a show to the world of seeking help for the troubled child, or make no bones about what she is doing to destroy her. There is nothing worse than having sticky-sweet, sick demons trying to cure you of a problem they themselves have caused.

Let us leave the variety of mother's teases for the reader's reflection; there is simply no end to her talent for confusing. But the goal is always the same: to upset and make the child doubt herself, to get something of the predator inside the victim, devouring her substance. The appropriate defense is also based on a consistent principle: see what it is they are up to, don't doubt yourself and remain calm and patient throughout all the trials that will befall you and you will survive your father-powered mother.

Now, let us assume instead that mother one day awakens to realize the error of her ways and repents. It is the child's turn to be threatened by mother's innocence. The mother's nature in the child, denied the reinforcement of mothering, will tease the parent back into her old role of witch. Whenever a parent's nature gets into a child, it aches for the corrupting influence to sustain it. The sick nature needs evil, phony love, and can literally thrive on downright cruelty.

Cruelty is the first tease which upsets and traumatizes the child. Then the same brand of cruelty becomes a kind of "love," a food, a reinforcement for its seed in the child. Cruel reinforcement for what cruelty planted is like love in that it nurtures the false identity. Without it, that identity begins to die. (Incidentally, a sense of dying is what you experience as you give up being teased and resentful, and

140

that is very good indeed.) We feel that cruelty is what we deserve because that is what we have grown to need, which is why we accept this sort of life.

Therefore, in the light of everything I have said, expect both you and your child to go through withdrawal symptoms. If you are a mother, expect to be teased, intimidated and rejected by your child, who is hoping that something in you will be called out of hell once again to play the role of tyrant, a tyrant of sickly affection or of meanness. Sons and daughters of witches need the tease in order to exist. But witches and offspring of witches must "die," if you are all to find who you really are.

If you are a reformed drunkard, expect to find your nag change roles and become the family lush. Would you believe that a woman can actually get high driving her old man to drink, nagging him to give up drinking—knowing all the time that she is making him worse with her nagging and pretentious concern?

No matter what kind of madness or sickness you have, expect the person behind the scenes of your dilemma (who up till now has been symptom-free, the one who was all worried about your health) to become sick—not with just an ordinary sickness, but with YOURS. This is all for the best, because once things are turned back around the right way, so that the real culprit gets back all the guilt feelings and anxiety that rightfully belong to him, maybe, *just maybe*, he or she will have a chance to repent and to change.

A great majority of psychiatrists are professional mothers; they have this same parent-child relationship with their wretched patients. Either the patient lays his sickness on the doctor (who becomes sick) or the doctor lays his sickness on the patient. *There is simply no other way it can be.* If the patient is more of a mother than the doctor, then he or she unloads the problem onto the psychiatrist; the doctor now needs therapy from another doctor. Pity the last momma-doctor on the top of the totem pole. Where does he go to unload his problems?

Generally speaking, modern medicine has become a surrogate mother to unsuspecting patients. Psychiatrists, especially, apply cruel, subtle principles of confusion and comfort. *Need is the love that is also hate.* Making patients need the services of the "good" doctor is the same as momma loving and unloading into her children. It is the way all those sick doctors remain "healthy." In this fashion, the psychotic patient becomes a psychotic receptacle for the sins of medicine. The doctor's pride is often threatened when the patient dies; he is just as angry when he finds the patient can make it without his "help."

In the same way, when a child dies or runs away, a mother has no one to take her guilt. You may have heard that being around children has a way of making a person feel young. This is because love and cruelty cause this exchange of power and identity to occur.

The doctor-patient relationship is rarely different from the mother-child one. A patient, having become corrupted by the doctor's comforting, grows to need the doctor, confusing his or her need with love. The doctor finds comfort in projecting, while the patient experiences the illusion which comes from the physician's reassuring presence. In love (involved) with his therapist, the victim is in therapy for ten, twenty, perhaps thirty years or more. He is a slave to therapy the way people are to drugs or alcohol—*all beginning with their mothers.*

142

By comforting the patient and seducing him to feel comfortable in his physical presence, the doctor plays the familiar trick of all guilt-ridden women. Comfort may feel good to the patient, but through the process of involvement, the patient actually takes on the doctor's problems and so the doctor "cures" himself. Treatment is really a selfish thing; the doctor's interest in the patient is really a roundabout self-interest.

It is not uncommon for a psychiatrist to give his patient sex-tease therapy to transfer his sin to his patient. The patient is taught to help her doctor to feel good about himself, receiving a reward for it. But the good feeling soon changes to guilt, driving her to love the doctor even more for the "cure." As the patient discovers a greater guilt, she associates the psychiatrist with relief. Again and again, the doctor rewards the patient for taking on his sin. The patient thrives on the doctor's phony concern; she feels guilt without it, yet becomes more guilty through it.

Not many people really want help. They like the way they are, but they don't like the way they feel (guilt). Now if you were a cannibal who felt guilty about being a cannibal and you went to your local witch-doctor shrink, he might console you or scold you, thus effecting a "cure" for you in a bizarre love-hate way. He might tell you, for example, that eating only six people in a month was the reason for guilt. You see, any good cannibal worth his salt eats TEN people a month, at least! Now you understand your problem: the guilt is not caused by being a degenerate cannibal but by not being a truly "fulfilled" cannibal! So, out you go, trying harder to fulfill your need to be a better cannibal, spurred on by the spirit of your witch doctor. You are very grateful to him for this service.

Evil, you see, always feels strengthened and refreshed by projecting its vile spirit; *it suffers a terrible sense of guilt when it fails to accomplish this goal.*

The ancient Israelites had a fascinating custom of unloading the burden of guilt by laying their hands on a goat—a scapegoat, it was called. When they had done their thing, they drove the wretched creature outside the city, cursing and spitting on it all the way and stoning it to death. This was their way of transferring the sins they had acquired—again, by transference.

In certain cultures, witch doctors have learned how to take on themselves the malevolent spirit of a person and its symptom sickness, then transfer it to the body of an animal, usually a chicken, which in turn is sacrificed. Some very interesting (but temporary) cures are effected in this way.

However, the ultimate transfer of the identity of sin and sickness takes place through the Messiah, the Savior of mankind. When He was here in the flesh, He took upon Himself the sins of His people, but without harm to Himself and without any need to pass it along to man or beast. The victim's sin was simply dissolved in the divine fire of His purity while the devotee received innocence *in exchange* for faith in Him. Remember the underlying principle, which is that there is *always* an identity exchange in identifying with good or evil. So, through identifying and believing *into* Him, we are forgiven and we experience an identity exchange. We lose the old spirit and receive a new nature. We lose the sinful spirit with its mortal nature and gain the immortal spirit and nature.

Through our parents, grandparents and all the way back to the original sin, the burden of sin has come down

144

to us. This problem of identity is where the problem lies for all of us. Fathers fail with their wives and mothers pass on to their children that original sin—plus some of their own.

You may be conditioned to feel holy, Christ-like, for taking the blame of your sick parents. In transferring their guilt, as they had to do in order that their egos might survive, your parents compounded their problem in you. If you are like most people, your parents set you up to feel responsible for what they did, to feel guilty for their perversity, drunkenness, illness, etc. You learned to be accepted by acting like a savior—but without any of His redemptive powers. You let people dump their burdens on you while they walked away feeling better. You got their blessing for being noble and accepting the blame. You associated "love" with being a successful scapegoat. Like it or not, you were stoned like a scapegoat; you became the whipping boy who took the punishment for the evils of your persecutors. Perhaps you feel that you have no right to speak up to stop this game; this is because, as an appeaser, your relief, your "righteousness" comes from catering to the needs of your tormentor.

But with God's Son, this sort of thing could never happen. For Him to take your sin upon Himself was like casting it into a purifying fire. Evil, sickness and sin were simply dissolved into the fire of His divine goodness, while He projected His divine Self to the repentant believer *in exchange for faith.*

Faith causes an exchange, whether it's faith in evil or faith in good. You see, the very purpose of worship is to identify with the object of worship in a right or a wrong way. Those people who put gods up on pedestals do so to become like gods themselves, to forget the guilt of such pride. Worship can be a way of becoming like a god in the forbidden sense, or of becoming Godly (a big difference!) in the redemptive sense.

Over and over, I have asked myself why I don't also take home the problems of those who seek my help. Recently, the Truth dawned on me. I was shown that it is because I have the spirit of His grace residing within me. And because of this, those who intuitively recognize this spirit can confess their sins and dissolve them in the Christ fire. But this purifying flame is not an external exchange as with temptation. It is simply caused by one awakened soul awakening another to the reality of God and Christ in themselves. To see and to acknowledge the Truth in another is the same as accepting that same spirit within yourself.

People worship deceivers, and because deceivers see and accept the worshipper as a god, the spirit of sin gets inside them through images of grandeur. This is what (the acceptance of) Christ saves us from. But let me warn you that you cannot find the Christ light by employing images, statues, crosses or ranting-and-raving preachers. These, my friend, are only more tricks. Salvation comes through realization, and realization through the stillness of a seeking soul.

You cannot manipulate or force the spiritual man (or woman) to be your savior/scapegoat. His sacrifice is a gift to the humble heart.

Some try to make me into a scapegoat. They try to put me on a pedestal or make me into a scapegoat as they have others. When they find they are unable to accomplish this, they are tormented throughout eternity or until they repent.

From now on it is no longer myself or you who are persecuted; it is they who are pursued and consumed, instead of saved, by the fire of our innocence.

In winter all trees may look alike. But when summer draws near, the live trees put forth leaves while the dead trees dry up and blow away.

The same Son (sun) gives you life or burns you alive.

If there is life in you, your soul is warmed by the awakening of this witness. No need to look outside for your identity anymore. You are becoming male or female once again. And, as the divine fire continues to grow in you, the Spirit of God will lead the man out of the male and the woman out of the female. And both shall one day stand on the approaches to Paradise and the Tree of Everlasting Life.

10: Causes and Prevention of Homosexuality

No matter how hard she tries, a woman finds it impossible to make her husband into a man. She can try being submissive and sweet; she can try being angry and resentful to make him measure up, but he only becomes more of a mouse or a rat—even a homosexual.

All that a woman's huffing and puffing can really do is make boys into women and girls into mommas, thus rewarding herself with a big case of frustration. At worst, her ambition can cause *her* to become the "man" of the house; her husband NEVER becomes the man she wants him to be!

No question about it, homosexuality is a mother/female induced illness, a condition transferred to succeeding generations through an emotionally charged climate of intrigue, violence and seduction.

Now let's set the record straight for homosexual sympathizers already bristling with defensive hostility. Your reaction indicates that you are either a latent homosexual or a mother-lover mother. Do I shock you? Well, let me remind you that shock is the name of the game of life. Bad shocks can make you sick, but good shocks could shock you into being well again. Read on! It is all quite shocking!

As I said, the hostile reaction proves I have struck a nerve. Go ahead, throw this in the wastebasket as proof that your corrupted nature can't bear the light of the truth about you and what you have done to others. Otherwise, what harm is there in reading on?

There's a strange thing about perverts and their creators: no matter how low they sink, no matter how fat they get or how much they stink, they want more than anything to be accepted as they are.

Perverts and fatsos resent the straight world because "straights" get jobs and seem to have all the fun; but for perverts and fatsos, the going is rough.

Many try to go straight or to get thin, but somehow they never make the grade. Rejected by the world, they are once again threatened. In desperation, there remains one thing to do—convince the world that "weird" (or fat) is beautiful. Fanatically, they press on and on, proclaiming the "good news" of salvation for all perverts and fatsos: "Fat is normal, fat is beautiful, fat is merely a preference," they cry. "If God had wanted us to be thin, He would have made us thin. God can't make mistakes and He made us the way we are!"

They make such a hullabaloo that other people begin to think *they* are weird for not accepting fatness (or perversion) as beautiful. Of course, they would be right if God had made perverts and gluttons, but He didn't. (However, another intelligence did.)

You name it—from "alcoholism is a disease" to "homosexuality is a God-given lifestyle, a sexual preference," all sick, troubled, guilty and degenerate souls are out to prove the world wrong about them. Unfortunately, in order to make themselves comfortable, they must now confuse people and make others feel guilty for rejecting them. It is not enough for sickos to accept one another; as long as there remains one sane, aware person, they will persecute that perceiving soul.

In the final analysis, there are two varieties of degenerates. One is so vain, so stubborn, so incorrigible that no matter how rotten, ugly or wrong he is, he must see himself as normal. If he is a cannibal, then he is not satisfied until all men are cannibals. His deviant and criminal mind is constantly scanning new ways to rationalize his condition, dredging up fiendish techniques of confusion to destroy the morals and the innocence around him in order to make the world "safe" for himself and his kind of creeps. All deviants—like cannibals—elect their idols to reinforce them individually; later, as a collective cannibal society, they have their kings. And, of course, wherever they can get away with it, "benevolent" perverts become despots creating laws forbidding *morality, honesty and innocence.*

On the other hand, there is the type of person who awakens to see what he has become, saying to himself, "What is wrong? I've got to find an answer." With this soul, no answer will do except the right one that will restore to him his lost dignity. This person doesn't want to change the world. He is troubled, however, by the support which comes from other homosexuals, cannibals, drunks and fatsos in general. He simply cannot accept his own sickness no matter what.

Some of you who have read this far, I can help. But, if you have only tolerated me this far to find fault, let me

150

warn you, *you won't*. You will, however, discover more horrible truths about yourself.

Now let me come back to the point where I said mother is the *cause* of homosexuality. I neglected to mention that the *fault* is father's weakness. It is only natural for children to be subject to the strongest emotional influence, so when man defaults on his spiritual obligations, woman becomes the authority in the home. The woman, as mother of man's fallen nature, must also be the whore that accepts its failing (lust) as virtue.

More often than not, a woman is possessed by a guileful nature. She wants this nature to be subdued by the love of a real man, but when her weak husband caters to that evil spirit in her (in the hope that she will support *him*), he falls under a spell. Whether she is an impatient, vile witch or a timid, submissive, clinging vine, the mother spirit is the dominant power in the home, sapping the strength of even a violent, macho man and his unprotected, unsuspecting brood.

Politicians are elected to be public servants, but because the guileful game they play draws strength from the weakness of the voters, they rise as hypnotic leaders of an impotent populace. The game is the same with "pubic" servants, as with "public" servants. Playing sexual politics, guileful women tantalize and emasculate their foolish husbands, thus stealing their authority.

It makes little difference whether our "pubic" servant is a vile, violent Hitler type or a "sweet" Hitler rising lovingly to every occasion like a Big Momma to soothe away pain; it makes no difference if she is pounded into the ground by a violent and rebellious husband and forced to do her "pubic" duty in meekness, fear and trembling—*a woman remains the basis of what "her" man is becoming.* And really, it is his own grievous fault.

Because of what his mother did to him, a man becomes either too fearful or too aggressive with women. In trying to prove his manhood with women, he becomes more and more of a woman himself because of them. Too much woman is as much the basis of male violence as it was the basis of his subservience. Having discovered the principle that "to serve is to rule," he then reduces his woman to the status of slave. In this violent way he *thinks* that he has taken the driver's seat and that he is "king of the mountain." But whether slave or servant (to a man's ego), *the female remains the base of what he is becoming*—helpless and mild, or a violent beast. Even a battered wife's ego may secretly enjoy the contempt she feels for the rat or mouse she has created.

Whatever the circumstances under which she "submits," whether to pleading or to force, the woman sustains man's mother-centered being; she services his agony and ecstasy, weakness and madness. "Love" sustains him one way; blame and hate sustain him in another; but the end result is always the same. The reason? *Man's ego was never created to be sustained by a woman's love!* This was never her proper role! He draws upon a legacy of tragedy when he teaches her to mother the lust of his fallen animal nature.

Whether her "love" results in weakness or in hate, she is the mother of terrible changes in him. Guilty and fearful of the power she has, she may attempt to return to him the responsibility (which he cannot handle). Then she learns that a woman cannot "elect a man to office"—and still have him be a man. The boss-maker is still the boss.

In order to become a real man, every male must discover how to prevent his wife from becoming his mother! There is something implanted in every female that wants to mother—even smother—him. Concomittantly, there is something in every male that responds and wants to be mothered. That "something" is pride, which keeps him changing and dying.

In employing her inherited "advantage," a woman tends to reduce a man to the status of a pussycat. Later on, giving up power in fear or guilt, she *herself* becomes the pussycat. She is the power behind both pussycats and violent beasts. As either the fearful psychotic or the violent beast, she has changed roles with the man. The beautiful world that might have been is lost; a jungle world of despotism arises from the ruins of Paradise.

In order to become suggestible, one must be excitable. The excitement which the male ego needs sets the stage whereon he gives the female power to lie to him. Gradually, she becomes him, a man in a woman's body, while the man becomes more like her inside himself. In order to keep the female from breaking out, he must rebel and compensate with great anger, like a ferocious animal—as a macho beast and not as a real man. Conquest by love is replaced by conquest by violence.

If a man cannot find his Ground of Being, he is subject to female influence. It is the lot of womanizers to become women or beasts. In all relationships that involve temptation and corruption, that subtle exchange of identity occurs where one becomes the other. The spirit of the lower realm ascends to incarnate itself first in the woman and then in the man, who assumes the woman's nature.

The debasement of male identity continues through

two basic, emotionally-loaded ego appeals:

1) The cruel tease

2) and the sexual tease.

The male ego is dependent on the excitement of tease. No tease, no excitement. No excitement, no tease. Where excitement is not present, man *looks* at woman in a way that excites him. A woman knows this look; it is the signal, the call to mother his nature.

Cruelty provides the irritation that satisfies the judging side of male pride, while the sexual tease ("love") satisfies its monarchic side. Every ego feels like God: that is, like king and judge. For example, when a man is just about to stand up to his wife's transgressions (the way a man should), she might say, "I want to go to bed and make love." There goes his authority! His ego finds it impossible to resist the ego-reinforcement of a subject's love—especially when he feels guilty for being upset with her. And, after he sees he has been tricked, he can't resist the tease to judgment.

Perhaps he is worried, preoccupied with important business matters—but not having all attention focused on *her* can threaten the (sick) female ego. So what does she do? She aggravates for attention, because she knows that when a man is upset, his soul will fall from grace and will then feed her sick need with sexual surrender or(failing that) the surrender of hate.

You see, a successful appeal to pride always stimulates the male sex drive, which makes the woman devilishly excited to take advantage; male desire means security to her, if a man has failed to love her properly. Her guileful

154

spirit becomes obsessed with feeding herself with his falling. When he finally becomes impotent, she is threatened and tries to solve this problem in different ways. One of those ways is with other men; this complicates her identity problem. Another is by aggravating the rest of the life out of his miserable carcass.

The male reaction to a female love/hate tease takes one of two forms:

> 1) He goes on submitting to both cruel and sexual provocation, just so long as she accepts his weakness as virtue; here his ego doesn't have to own up to any fault.

> 2) He compensates, through violence, for the wrong of failing. Anger happens to be a wrong man's way of looking strong and right in his own eyes; amazingly, the same illusion of being strong and right can arise from being "loved" and accepted.

No matter how he tries to degrade a woman through sex and violence to raise his self-image, her spirit gets inside him; rebellion is another form of conformity. Both her tease and reward serve the mother-lust in him for power, and with this power she teases for more power. A man can become addicted to a woman's nagging to justify even his rebellion, his sense of machismo, just as he can become dependent on her "love" for his reassurance. But remember this basic principle:

> *You become like what you hate, just as you become like what you love.*

In either way, a man becomes addicted to the ego-reinforcing mother-female presence, while he *becomes* her, internally.

Why do you think macho men spend hours at boxing, wrestling or lifting weights? Mostly, they are trying to compensate for the mother nature within them. Alas, no sooner do women admire them for their beautiful forms or accomplishments, than, lo and behold, there is more female inside. Truly, it is a vicious, endless cycle.

A successful man is just as much, if not more, in danger of becoming a homosexual as his failure counterpart. Why is this?—you may well ask. Again, the answer is to be found in looking at the principle of the ego-support of corruption. Ambitious (wrong), proud, vain men cannot stand alone without the female reassurance of (mother) love. As men "succeed," they experience conflict. The more anxious they feel about woman-motivated achievement, the more they need a woman to soothe away the pain. Here again, the mother spirit gets inside a man's ego via sexual reinforcement.

Remember, the sex act per se is not necessarily a reinforcement for a man's ego, any more than food should be, but when sex does become an ego-reinforcement, then a change of identity (id-entity) occurs.

Man is a religious being, a creature of spiritual identity who cannot exist long without a sense of belonging, without reflecting the god of that longing and belonging. So, as man-fallen-from-grace is reassured by woman, he eventually reveals who has become the ground of his being. This sort of thing is a very real danger in every home where woman is the ministering angel of sympathy and support. If a man is unaware, he gets sucked in and altered. He pays the penalty of pride and sin with his life—even his soul.

Perhaps you can see the reason why certain women find homosexuals interesting and attractive. In every weak, effeminate man lives the mother spirit. A woman can serve her momma in him, or dominate momma in him. A weak or vicious male also provides her with a carcass to hate and to use the way her mother used her father.

Momma is everywhere, inside women, outside women, inside men. The mother spirit is honored by weak and effeminate men. "Men" are also excited by the momma with a muscle-bound, fleshly, machismo casing around it. And a woman who marries such a man may believe that she has escaped her mother at last, and found a real man! Alas, her mother's spirit has beguiled again. The female with the masculine identity is deceived by the muscle with the female identity.

When an emotionally sick man has sex, it is similar to a woman having sex with another woman. This is so much the case that, with a sexually-exchanged couple, the female who has become a male feels lust and burning the way a man does. She can actually feel like a man having sex with a woman. Soon, the woman "evolves" more feeling than the man does, and the retiring, effeminate male begins to feel less and less excitement, deriving "his" pleasure from being the one pursued, creating the aggravation and tease. There are so many perversions. Follow any one of them to its ultimate conclusion— decay, corruption and death.

Think of it as the female spirit in a man, reaching out for the demon mother-spirit of love, and eating out his substance. As he ceases to exist as a male he becomes unable to deliver up to her his male essence to feed her ego because he is too much like a woman.

Now what does he do? For a woman, there would be a latent pattern of lesbianism here, but before fulfilling it, she might try other men, hoping to find the correcting love she needs. All she would get is more of the same sexual use, while momma (in her) would keep feeding on that loathsome masculine substance.

Remember the principle of exchange which exists through the terrible tease of cruelty and seduction. Our entire being senses the principle of our demise in this way: If we can lose something of ourselves, our identity, through being teased and through sexual corruption, then perhaps we can regain that identity by applying the same method in reverse. With this principle as the evolved but unconscious driving force, the sexually-exchanged man, unable to relate to a woman (because he is so much like one himself) turns on to men. It is simply a matter of regressive evolution—*evil*ution and *devil*ution. A man simply starts tempting other men—or he tempts women *trying to get his own back*.

Allow me to cite a typical example of this. A husband and wife fight. He becomes violent. Obviously he looks like the bad guy; she looks hard-done-by. Their son, watching all of this emotional interplay, rejects his father and "accepts" his mother. Later in life he discovers his mother's identity inside of him. Now, he also sees how mother's spirit tricked him to accept her nature, and he resents her for that. The resentment reinforces her spirit within him.

By now the son has become a woman's man. He tries to be a man by having sex with women. But the woman who makes him feel like a man only puts more woman-ishness into him, in the usual way (sex). So, to offset this, he may have sex with men because the female inside teaches him how to excite and to be excited in order to get his masculinity back.

Now his mother tries to help him, but she is too strong, and talks *at* him, which makes him resent her all over again. As he resents, the woman in him flowers anew and he feels the urge for experiences with men. It is a vicious cycle.

Some homosexuals seek the love of a father, but the only way that "manhood" can rub off (so to speak) is through the excitement and intrigue of sexual exchange. After all, such a male is a female, having learned his ways from his mother or from sexual experiences with women. Consequently, acting like a female, he tries to get his own male identity back. The female in him aggravates, teases and excites the other man, as he tries to change or to get back some of that man's essence.

A female with a male identity does the same thing. She hopes to get her female identity back by trying to be more of a woman, exciting weak and effeminate men to feel like men. Naturally, it backfires. She becomes more of a man inside.

The male who plays the homosexual's "father" role is an imposter. He—rather *she*—is another troubled soul also trying to become a man by seeking a (female) child to accept him as a father. This is the classic combination of an effeminate person seeking his identity from another "man." Deep down inside they are both women becoming devils; homosexuals, too, exchange identities.

But then there is the real, dyed-in-the-wool homosexual

"mother" who is *not* seeking his identity back; he/she simply digs in and consolidates "itself" in the male body. This evil spirit, having enslaved the soul, loves being a "mother" in its male "house." This perverted male revels in the *power* that females have by virtue of their sex. The female demon in this male body continues seeking revenge against mankind, delighting in their destruction through all sorts of perversions.

If it is true that the human psyche becomes imprinted through trauma, and if there was an original sin, then we should expect to find the female identity transferred to men even to this very day.

If it is true that the basis of the original trauma was pride, we should also expect to see this weakness passed down to all men. And if it is the nature of pride to maintain wrong as right, then you would expect pride to subsist on a steady diet of lies.

If these lies cause change, then we should expect to see degeneration in mankind, sustained by deceit.

And if lies cause trauma and sustain changes, then we should expect to see more and more of the female nature inside men. Look around: doesn't that explain the prevalence of homosexuality in men?

Let's run that through again: let us call the pride in man a weakness. Surely, the cure for pride's failing would lie in owning up to that weakness—but then how could a man go on being proud? He couldn't! To go on being proud is the same as needing and being sustained by bigger and bigger lie-producing traumas. Lies, traumas and change must then become a man's lifestyle, far different from what it might have been.

Now, if Adam and Eve were the first living beings, and

if the entire human race descended from them, we should expect to find this prideful nature working in men and women today, and we should expect to find the same problems between them.

If the corrupted have descended to depend upon the source of their change, then it follows that we should expect to find a male weakness for the mother-spirit of its fallen existence, rising as a mothering spirit.

If it is true that there is a good and an evil way, if it is true that pride causes one to fall to the lower way, then we should expect to find the prideful male addicted (to the female/mother), and he would call his addiction "love."

All of this is written to show you that the need which troubles you so much is not love, that if you could only find it in your heart to let your perverted needs pass, you would not miss anything. You would certainly not die. But, if you do *not* let them pass, you most certainly *will* die. And while you may feel that you are dying as a result of denying your false self that false need, you will, in reality, be coming alive in the way you have forgotten.

Do you, as a man, lust unnaturally for women—or for men? Let those lusts pass. If you seek to regain your lost masculinity through such experiences, you will surely lose it forever. Do you, as a woman, burn like a man? This is the male identity in you seeking the female-mother in the male. Let that desire pass. Fail in this and you will reinforce the mother in your man and the man in yourself.

Let pass all these abominable needs, so that the sick nature in you will die and the *real* you will be established, eternally renewed by God's grace. *Be still, and understand that you cannot recover your lost identity by any other means than this.*

Understand that your perverse, craven need to seek your lost dignity through people is nothing but an infant evil, crying out for the mother of its existence. Then starve that mother of need and need for mother. Starve her outside; starve her inside. Observe her calmly and objectively in her need, and in her need to be needed.

SEEK, THEREFORE, SALVATION *FROM* THE MOTHER IN THE WOMAN...AND THE MOTHER IN YOURSELF.

11: The Power of Emotionless Love

One of the most dangerous things you can do to a child's mind is to attempt to mold his character. In fact, everything that is wrong with us stems from others' shaping influences on our minds in our formative years. If only we knew how to be ourselves, there could be no unsolvable problems. Conflicts have arisen and problems have appeared just from not being ourselves. It is just that simple!

So the question arises, how did we forget to be ourselves? And the answer is: because of the pressure and the corruption of a childhood conditioning process—"culture," in other words. Culture is like a prevailing disease against which the individual must become uniquely immune if he is to survive. This may come as a surprise to you, but the hand that rocks the cradle also holds the key to the perpetuation of culture.

Children were not designed to be performing circus beasts, conditioned by trainers for the pleasure-taking of the system. They are little people, whose rights and spiritual needs must be properly understood and fulfilled. Now, I am not saying that parents should give up disciplining their children. I *am* saying that parents should remember that children are people, not beasts. Children differ from the wild beasts in that they have souls; thus, different rules must apply in rearing them.

A different kind of love than that which brings children into the world is required if you are to bring up an emotionally stable family. Animal "love" merely procreates animal bodies, but Divine love breathes life into the souls which live in them.

Superhuman perception, energy and endurance are needed if you are to bear the outrages of other egos. Survive the ravages of your mother, your marriage partner and your kids, and you will surely know the meaning of happiness. Just think of it this way: without mad bulls there would be no good matadors. The point is that unless you learn to properly cope with the cruel stresses of life, you cannot grow in understanding.

It is the father's duty to lead his entire family to the Divine Source of their existence. Woman is only the source of the fallen, natural existence. Uncanny wisdom must be applied in dealing with her. Improperly regarded, she can be as lethal as a poisonous snake; loved and understood, she can be more precious than rubies.

The mother as lover and central figure in the home is a manipulator, seducer and destroyer who knows not what she does.

Children depend on mother's warmth and charms to sustain their "rising fallen natures" which she gave them. But at a certain phase, father is duty-bound to save them from her clammy, "loving" grasp. It is *father* who should be lover and center of family fascination, not mother. Everything should revolve around him; if it doesn't, God help you!

Unlike the lower animals, man has two natures, which war with each other for ascendancy. This dual nature must be considered in rearing children.

A body is born from a body, and a spirit from a spirit. All newborn infants arrive through mothers by way of nature, conceived through fathers' inherent weakness for mothering. Children of men are first natural creatures, but they can go on to mature into spiritual beings.

It is only through being sincerely committed to family life that married men discover truth more deeply, which enables them to conquer their weakness for women. Slowly but surely, men must outgrow their carnal need for female reassurance; they must learn to fail less with them. A failing man cannot become a woman's authority; nor can he implant his good father image in his male children, or set the stage for his female offspring to attract strong, noble men.

The process of becoming a really good parent is in itself a growing-up experience. As you correct your child, the naughty child in you is loved. Unfortunately, most parents have had little, if any, corrective love in their formative years. They bring with them into marriage the hell of *their* parents and various childish, selfish cravings. More often than not, a man is just another child to his wife, competing with the baby for momma's affections—a spoiled brat, teasing his wife (the way he did his momma) to let him have his own way. When husbands and wives are immature, they are on the same emotional level as their children, so they are not only involved with their own childish intrigues with one another, but with their children's sniveling rivalry as well! So, everyone in the family continues to evolve madly and wildly against the

Spirit, and there exists no referee, no modifying factor of Divine authority in the home. That is what is behind all family tragedies.

It is the male ego-weakness, seeking love, which tempts the female to take over and become the power. Female domination sets little girls up to seek weak men (like their fathers), and male children to seek dominating wives (like their mothers), so that original sin perpetuates itself through succeeding generations of hell on this wretched earth.

Because of the duality of earth and heaven in their natures, children need two kinds of sustaining love:

First, they need sensual affection from mother.

Second, they need the ultimate love — agape', or Godly, fatherly love — to save them from the curse concealed in smother-love.

Father-love must override and correct excessive female doting. Mother's emotional love, if not eventually modified by father's emotion*less* love, overdevelops the child's prideful ego and eventually ruins the child, who came into the world by the seduction of the father.

While female love may be the kind that makes the world go 'round, it is also the kind that destroys it. While sensuous love is needed for one phase of (animal) growth, it must be transcended to attain the next. In order to save his children from their mother, a man must first discover how to save himself *from his wife.*

Children need some kind of ego reassurance to help them physically mature toward the threshold of Reality. First a child grows in the ego way; later, he is supposed to

166

develop humility. But most of us don't even know what that second way is. So we grow up—and then down—with a woman's loving help; we continue to perpetuate the misery of our "birth-wrong." For no apparent reason (because we are so unaware), we feel guilty, self-conscious and inferior.

Even if we do realize that mother's uncorrected, unloved spirit is operating behind the scenes, there is little we can do. Tradition has granted her—like it or not—the role of lover and despot. Women-libbers notwithstanding, motherhood is still looked upon with misguided worship in our culture. But it is actually a mysterious psychotic weakness which causes man to embrace the evil in the woman rather than the woman herself—which makes her into a devil.

An understanding of our origin is needed if we are to avert our prideful destiny—suffering, tragedy and death. The lie stands at the beginning of life as we know it, and false love brings us to the end; false love is part of the conspiracy of the lie.

Love is from a god, for a god. Man's need for a woman makes the woman his god. Man that is born of woman is created in *her* image and *her* likeness, and is dependent on *her* reassuring, loving presence. This may very well be animal life—but it also happens to be the life which leads to spiritual death.

The guile which originates with woman is the world's most powerful and destructive hypnotic force. Any man who hopes to become a leader of men must be a female at heart. Watch the seductive powers of popular politicians as they fascinate, lie-love and bamboozle the masses for votes. Remember, love is from a god and for a god! Therein lies the secret of Satan's power.

The earthy, sustaining love which all prideful people need—not true love at all—is as vital to them as food. But, there must come a day when love will drive both the woman who provides it and the man who receives it into the common madness!

Ego-selfhood develops naturally from its relationship with mother, but a fatherly warmth is desperately needed to help every child transcend the death grasp of a female "god," earth-life giver—and life taker. ("God" giveth and "god" taketh away!)

It is a very unusual child indeed who can survive his mother without a father's love. In search of love, children will sell their souls. A mother whose son had turned to homosexuality once told me of the time her son screamed with agony at his weak, unhearing, uncaring father, "I became a homosexual because I was looking for a father!"

Until he is saddled with the responsibility of raising a family, a man can avoid facing his weakness. But once "safely" inside the prison walls of family life, he sees who is *really* in charge. Up to that point he lives in a fool's paradise, dreaming that he is "into" something which he is not, assisted by his perverted helpmate/playmate.

Everyone despises a weak father, even those who pretend to love him (in order to use him). Because of his weakness, he is unfaithful, and his children go astray, while his wife is driven to other men, seeking love she will never find. Soul mates outside marriage turn out to be cell mates. For "good behavior" there is "reprieve" from marriage—but never from the lower kind of hell.

Gentlemen of the Light, seek the ideal of which I

speak, or else suffer the hell of a second fall—for living with a woman without true love *is* pure hell.

Observing the wreckage of your own and your children's lives should sober you and drive you to seek the answer. No wonder you feel guilty and responsible! Of course you wring your hands in desperation! Of course you long for an opportunity (that may never come) to do it over again!

Immaturity and selfishness in dealing with your family have caused you to miss the boat as far as your own spiritual development is concerned. But hold on! Don't despair! There *is* a way out. And it has something to do with looking at love in a different light!

Remember that need is the only kind of love a man has to give. And remember, too, that love is for a god and from a god. Through your inherited but unholy need for ego support, look who has become your god now! (Or should I say, look at who *are* your *gods*.)

The only love a person can feel is *need*. And need is an anxiety which can be fulfilled in a right way or a wrong way. To need a woman is to be fulfilled in an infantile, dead-end, egocentric way. Good or bad, all love is need, but *true* love becomes a burning bush, a fire that is enduring and overwhelming. The fire in Moses' burning bush had its own (invisible) fuel source which was not the bush: it burned and was not consumed.

Seek, then, that indwelling, eternal energy source. Fuel your love with life from within. A candle burns from the melted wax rising up the wick. Without wax, the wick burns out. Take heed, therefore, that you do not burn yourself out living from the energies of your own love/ hate and frustration. Alas, without "the fuel from within,"

169

you are bound to burn the energy of the wicked itself. You burn yourself out; you burn out your family.

You came into this world with just so much life-force. When that energy is spent, you find yourself at the end of your rope—and of your life. Be careful how you react: don't give your energy to sin, to false gods, in your hunger for approval and devotion.

Every man born of woman feels anxious and self-conscious, and each makes the same fatal mistake of crawling inside a woman—like the worm he is—in order to resolve his conflict.

Every woman feels a man's abuse, and each man gets to feel her use of his abuse; they end up blaming and hating each other.

Fallen man seeks to vindicate an ancient guilt through the love of a beautiful woman, but her love only aggravates his problem with himself. His ego then tries to resolve this conflict in two wrong, guilt-producing ways:

He blames her.

He uses her again.

His bewildered ego makes the fatal mistake of seeking "innocent" solace in a woman's guile. Then he justifies that mistake by hating her treachery.

The earth-bound ego receives its pleasures through love/hate escapes and is sustained by the energies that are released through excitement. Reacting with "love" and hate, it sucks everyone into a reciprocal and hypnotic love/hate relationship. Children will reflect, imitate and react to parental emotions and attitudes.

Anxiety over what you are (especially over what you

have become through hate) causes you to need more love. That is what makes you obligate your children to respect you. Sometimes they do—and sometimes they hate you instead. This is the basic pressure which destroys you and yours.

All feelings are selfish. No guilty, dying soul can feel alive without some feeling of emotion. If it is denied love, then hate will do just as well.

Emotion is the chief "commodity" of selfishness. For the ego to survive apart from God, it must create scenes during which it can "trade" emotions. I ask you, how can you give the gift of selfhood and independence to your child when you are selfishly and emotionally involved in making your child into a violent beast or a warm puppy, enslaving him to your sick ego needs?

Are you an angry person? Then you teach your child resentment. He grows up like a wild beast with an insatiable appetite for judgment. You both get to look at each other's faults—to keep from seeing your own! And the same is true of the wrong kind of love. You either make your child into a lover and a slave of love, or into a hater and a slave of hate.

Satisfying your own selfish ego-need, you project your own prideful identity, setting your children up for a future love/hate, intrigue-filled, dog-eat-dog existence in which nothing grows but pride, conflict and tragedy.

In order to stand in correction to another, you must exemplify the quality you wish to develop. Exemplifying humility does not project change the way that pride does, through emotion-based mimicry—a monkey see, monkey do sort of thing. No, the magic of a good example is much more profound than that. You accomplish this marvelous thing by being as conscious as you want others to be. In other words, it is more an *awakening* experience than a learning one.

The kind of love of which I speak needs no emotional support from anyone; it is fully capable of freeing others from the vicious, slavish obligation to return love or hate. If "love" or hate should arise, as is their habit (perhaps as manipulative ploys against you), then your patient awareness does not return feelings. Instead it neutralizes and frees the "lover" or hater from his compulsive behavior toward you.

The greatest of all gifts (especially appropriate at Christmas time) is choosing *not* to give, which frees others from the obligation to give something in return for what you've given them. Being obliged to give binds others to the agony of giving. Do you see what I mean? Giving under pressure wrongly resolves a conflict that was implanted by suggestion. In effect, the pressure source is rewarded and the giver can become a pressure source to others. The pressure that makes you "give" becomes the pressure that makes others "give," too. The same principle applies to your love needs for your children.

Although children are indeed emotionally involved with their parents, parents must never be involved with them. That is how you reveal your love to your children: by not playing the emotional game. Children sense any parental ego-weakness toward them and are tempted to exploit this emotional bond. But if they find calm parental strength instead, it relieves them. Why? Because emotionless love doesn't tempt, and cannot be tempted to tempt.

Without the love which comes through the unselfish emotionless state, your need compels you to respond and to cause others to respond endlessly to you with love and hate. Like it or not, you reinforce one another's ego madness. The worst in others evolves to become an even worse part of you, and the worst in you becomes an even more sick part of them.

No one in his wrong mind has any Divine Love to give. Even if one did have love, the wrong mind would not give it, because its expression would eliminate the basis of the ego's own selfish and prideful existence.

Emotion in all its forms, passing back and forth between people, evolves beasts and demons, but *never* human beings. If the world became perfect tomorrow, few people could stand the pain. Our sick egos engineer problems: problems challenge and excite our sick souls to grow, to forget the guilt of growing in that way.

Have you any idea how much guilt is behind the love you think you feel for others? Tell me, have you ever successfully made up to anyone without setting the stage for being betrayed, used and upset all over again?

Cupid shoots his poisoned arrow of emotion straight into the ego's heart. *Agape'*—emotionless—love *alone* is the antidote.

Submissive love, the kind that weak, guilt-ridden men feel for their mothers, wives and children, is not really love at all. It is a form of slavery, motivated by the need to soothe guilt, anxiety and hate.

It is commonplace to see an apparently decent, thoughtful, highly-principled male provider whose wife and children walk all over him. To add insult to injury, they may even resent the helpless fool for not being the man in charge.

A weak father places his family under a compulsion to

take over *and this is the problem he ends up battling.*
When resentment produces a show of violent strength,
he finds *that* emotion to be his next undoing. His alterna-
tives are between the devil and the deep blue sea: that is,
to be more submissive, or more violent. Feeling guilt for
his violence makes him afraid of being upset, which fear
is the impetus for being wishy-washy again. This in turn
leads his family to take more liberties—fill in your own
variation and unhappy ending.

Father feels guilty for his "love" and hate; mother feels
guilty *from* his love and hate, and for her own love and
hate. The children feel betrayed; they acquire guilt from
the license they are given to take liberties, and then from
the violent suppression of their transgressions. They
develop their own love/hate thing: love weak daddy/hate
weak daddy; love weak mommy/hate weak mommy.

It is not the children's fault that they are wild, and it is
not (usually) the woman's fault that she is a nag, mad
with power or driven to drink.

**It is a man's lack of commitment to what is
right—his lack of courage to resist what his
selfish ego needs—that is the real problem.**

I am reminded of an old saying: "when the cat's away,
the mice will play"—meaning, of course, that in the
absence of authority you will find chaos. It is not so much
that women and children are bad; it is rather that men are
weak. It is in the nature of little egos to go astray in the
absence of authority and to behave well in its presence.

Children need authority. If children are not guided by
the presence of good authorities, they will be influenced
by bad ones. Evil simply fills the vacuum left by a lack of

guidance. If you do not claim them with emotionless love, the devil in their mother will seduce them with her emotional appeal.

Observe how difficult it is to stand against those you need. You are obliged to be weak with those from whom you need support or they will pull the rug from under your wobbly ego. So, gentlemen, look ahead to your inevitable end and choose sides: woman-approval or Divine-approval. Build your house on sand or on rock; a womanizer can hardly enter the Kingdom of God.

Pity the families of weak men. There are millions of them, all going to rack and ruin, sustained in their meaningless existence by the gutless, emotionally angry, emotionally submissive fathers. Here is where the suffering begins and here is where it must end.

Where there is none of the strength which comes from knowing, failing comes to take its place. Where there is failing, there also is emotion; emotion is the stuff of which the evolution of hell-on-earth is made.

Let me frame what I just said in a different way. Suppose President Reagan and President Carter were to take a stand on exactly the same issue involving a Communist act of aggression. Chances are that the Communist world would back down if Reagan were President. Egocentric nations behave just like little kids, compelled to take advantage *only* when they sense their adversary's weakness. The principle is the same: to avoid war we need a *strong "father" president;* to avoid family strife, a strong father, rather than one who desires popularity, is also necessary. *Realize that your own ego-need for support represents a sin, a guilt, which you must learn to resolve in a right way.*

Remember, gentlemen, your weakness is really another form of wickedness. Men have a weakness for wickedness; wickedness rises to the call of weakness. When weakness reigns, men become fools and women become devils in disguise.

Weakness embraces wickedness. Weakness draws evil into existence to sustain it in its pride. Weakness, becoming wickedness, cannot properly oppose what it needs. Whenever it does oppose, power still goes to the tyrant to become more wicked, thereby at least sustaining the weak one in the illusion of his own goodness. When the weak go to "holy" war against the wicked, guess what happens when they win? *They become the very thing they opposed.*

Your submissive weakness draws up the problem you are forced to deal with violently. You are just as damned when you "win" the war as when you lose.

False love (appeasement) always causes aggressiveness, violence and war. True peace emanates from the strength that comes from the deep knowledge of what is right (faith), *never compromising or backing down for any reason whatsoever.*

Be sure of yourself in each emotionless moment. Stand calmly and fearlessly for what you know is right, against all doers, big and small; by so doing you will nip all problems in the bud. Abandon all care of losing love; abandon all thought of gaining love. Bear persecution graciously.

Any psychotic, friendly, nice, easy-going, submissive, people-appeasing mannerisms you have betray where you are coming from. It's just as though you stand around with a big sign on you which says: "I am a pushover, please take advantage of me!" Look how indignant you become when someone does—but look at how you really love it! Hating wrong is the only way your sick, weak soul has of being right. You compare yourself with the very wickedness that you have encouraged to serve your needs: first for love, then for judgment. Love and hate both reinforce the self-righteous ego monster within you.

Because they both support your ego, love and hate have a way of making you feel wrong any way you slice it, even when you are "right." A serving "demon" can make you feel guilty for accepting her "love." You will also feel guilt for failing to stand up in principle; then resentment takes over. Love a demon or hate a demon and you become a demon. Love a woman or hate a woman and you become a woman. The woman becomes your god and the demon in the woman is the god of both of you. And all this love/hate involvement stifles any meaningful change.

Righteousness based on hate makes you guilty; then guilt can confuse you and make you back down when you should fight. You might fight when you are wrong, or when you are right "in the letter," but only with the spirit of rage, not with the Spirit of Love. Backing down encourages others to take advantage; pushing too hard, forcing a point, breeds rebellion. The real answer lies in dealing with all emotional attacks with calm, patient, emotionless love.

Emotion is the life, breath, "righteousness" and strength of fools. If emotion doesn't make you forceful, mean and violent, then it drains away your strength as the emotion of love also drains you. If you don't explode and hurt others, you *im*plode and hurt yourself. But imploding fuels *all* problems, inside and out. And everything rotten in the world is glorified and justified through expressed (or repressed) love and hate. Everything you do under the spell of emotion is wrong. Everything you do or say in calmness is right. One way you can do no right; the other way you can do no wrong.

Clearly it is folly to struggle with the apparent problem. Address yourself to your own internal problem of self-doubt and moral cowardice. "Mr. Nice Guy," come out from behind your phony image and fight the good fight! As long as you have that silly ego-need to be popular with momma, you cannot fight for her. Eventually you end up fighting against her to keep her from eating you alive! But in the emotionless, selfless, loving war-to-end-all-wars, there are no losers: she wins if you win!

Mr. Nice Guy, you tend to overlook faults instead of taking a strong stand, because it is more important to you to be liked than to be principled. *You cannot be right and remain popular!* No matter what the issue is, right threatens all egos. And the feedback or lack of it threatens *your* ego because it doesn't get the support it is accustomed to in order to feel secure.

Sinners sympathize with one another in their common weakness and wickedness. Prideful egos are afraid of a better world (or better children) because good conditions do not excuse or sustain their own "beautiful" wickedness. Force an ego to face itself and God! How it hurts! And how you are blamed and hated for inflicting what feels like harm. Careful, don't hate back!

Guilty people experience pain in the presence of another's innocence, and that often makes them hate the innocent, as though *they* were doing something wrong by

178

making the guilty feel their guilt.

Children are not perfectly innocent—they are only relatively innocent compared with their sick parents. For this reason the most sensitive child in the family is inevitably singled out and degraded, often driven to alcohol, drugs and insanity.

Sickness demands the support of other sick people. Sick and evil people will make others sick and evil for the relief of guilt and the fulfillment of emotional need. They punish those who are true to themselves. Weak people cannot survive without a base in the wicked, and the wicked cannot survive long without exploiting the weak. That theme bears repeating over and over again.

The cannibal king is the lowest man in a cannibal culture. He is revered because he embodies and sustains everything that is cannibal. Now do you see why you draw the wrong types to you, why you elect all the wrong people to power?

Parents, watch your mood. Nothing threatens a child's well-being as much as observing a weak parent dragged to his knees by the evils and the stresses of life. Your depression, martyrdom, or fear of sickness is an example which tempts your child to hate you for being so miserable. He feels what you feel and is threatened by your weakness and sickness. He wants to run away from your gutless, morbid, pathetic, sticky, sympathy-seeking self. If he stays, it is only out of insecurity and guilt, which renders him helpless and submissive.

The sick parental identity is transmitted to the child through the child's own resentment and it can make him feel that his only hope of ever feeling happy or getting well is to stay around to help his miserable, sick, drunk or hypochondriacal parent. A classic scenario is reenacted when a child feels obligated to cure his parent's sickness with "love"—and the parent becomes worse. Once again the child is threatened; once again he feels resentment and guilt. Guilt binds him eternally to the agony of "saving" his parent in order to save himself. It is like sinking deeper and deeper into a swamp.

Dear children everywhere, *you cannot save your parents with self-sacrifice.* Nor do you have any moral obligation to do this sick and morbid thing. Your parents' only hope of salvation lies in your desire *not* to help them with the same kind of sick, dependence-creating "love" with which they crippled you. Until you realize this fact deeply, you can never get your own "act" together. Knowing the Truth will free you from the love/hate obligation trap.

Any false belief can cause emotion to rise, and emotion, in turn, reinforces that false belief. Similarly, a parent's failing causes emotion in a child. This emotion communicates the parent's egocentric condition to the child, along with the lie that the child is responsible for the parent and must save the parent with sustaining "love." Rubbish! Can't you see that this love is motivated by resentment-based guilt, that it destroys what it ought to preserve? The principle is the same for children who want to help their parents as it is for parents who are compelled to "help" their children with phony "love."

You will hear the unrighteous (who deserve to suffer) crying, hoping to solicit pity through your reaction. Pity, while making you feel important, enslaves you to lifting wretched spirits. Beware of the subtle pressure which contains a hidden ego-appeal. The tempting plea is

"Save me, O God! If You won't, who will?" *Don't fall for it!* It is Lucifer's way of pulling you in, keeping you in this hell on earth until he can take you to his abode *beneath* it! It is a temptation for you to appoint yourself as a responsible god. If you relieve the pressure of temptation in this wrong way, by serving them (getting a brownie button for your weakness), they may get better—only to sicken again later, upsetting you into feeling even greater responsibility for the guilt of "helping" them in the first place.

Remember, *all* emotion tempts you to feel emotional, to feel what others feel, to think what others think, so much so that you will be forced to live out another's will.

If you want to become a true lover of parents and of children, you must transcend pride with its base in love and hate. God will reward your abstention from emotional junkfood and fulfill you with His abiding strength and power.

There are more ego-emotional appeals on hell's earth than you can shake a stick at. Reject them all. Meet cruel emotion (which was designed for no other purpose than to upset you and make you doubt yourself) with calmness and without judgment. Do the same when faced with emotional praise, when others try to overwhelm you with phony emotional love—once again, to make you doubt yourself.

When people degrade you, simply see (from the non-emotional distance between you) that this is what they are trying to do. See also that they are using both pleasant and unpleasant emotion to distract you from your unbearably clear perception of them. See them trying to satisfy a selfish need with your emotional reactions. Whichever way you react, with love or with hate, you can never make them truly happy. Free yourself from them and free them from you by practicing unemotional love.

The need to feel emotion is as primitive, as ancient as original sin itself. Were the death-centered ego unable to feel emotion, it would not know it was alive; it could not survive. Witness people gravitating toward music, drugs, excitements and pleasures of all kinds which make them feel alive for illusive moments, but which in reality slowly drain them of their life and strength. Were they to awaken from their emotional stupor, they might realize how much more dead than alive they have become. But those who are too prideful to face up to their folly need emotion to help them forget that they are dying.

Emotions communicate lies to the ego, and the dead and dying are terribly afraid of meeting those who are living without emotion, in faith. They will try everything in their power to draw you into the emotional experiences *they* need, by "killing" you. If you do not give off the emotion they are looking for, and if, with patience, you neutralize whatever feeling they have left, then all they will have left to look at is their own wrong!

Through the meditation taught by the Foundation of Human Understanding, you can find the attitude (more an "altitude") of no attitude, the belief of not believing, the power of no power, the fight of no fight, the love of no love, the goodness of no goodness—even the hate of no hate. You will learn to put a distance, a space between yourself and others across which no emotion can pass, no evil enter. You will stand, observant, compassionate, but no longer subject to rage, to false sympathy or pity, to the feelings that have ruled you.

And from you only good shall go forth.

182

12: Fathers: Forgive Them, For They Know Not What They Do

You may be playing with fire if you seek to confront an angry parent with his past failings and cruelties toward you; for while you, the victim, can remember each episode down to the last gory detail, your violator has probably forgotten all about it. You may literally be taking your life in your hands if you try to face your tormentor before you are properly prepared, mentally and spiritually.

There are times when the only prudent way to deal with an "incurable" parent is to turn your back, walk out of his or her life, and never look back: Sometimes, the loneliness of time and distance will bring the angry one to his senses; if not, nothing is lost.

Most of us, however, do have an opportunity to return to the "scene of the crime," and face our parents with their past misconduct. In truth, your life could depend upon a successful outcome. But that is not to imply that your parents must necessarily see and admit to their past failings and make peace with you. Your salvation can not depend on such an admission. In fact, you will find only pain and frustration, with no hope of deliverance, should you foolishly feel compelled to make your parents "see the light." You must not try to save them as a roundabout way of saving yourself. Save yourself from that horror! Realize that your intensified sense of responsibility toward them has grown out of your guilt for having hated them.

By "successful outcome," I mean to say that you must face their inevitable assault on your efforts to clear the air without angrily putting them down or backing down yourself. You must approach them with neutral "feelings," without hate or judgment in your heart. Be prepared to forgive; or rather, to acknowledge your forgiveness, for you should already have forgiven them in order to arrive at that purified state of consciousness that enables you to confront them boldly, without fear. In that neutral state, you can speak truth with love, without hypocrisy, and without fear of the onslaught of recrimination that is almost certain to come.

Prepare for a hailstorm of verbal abuse. Stand tall, remain firm in your resolve; observe calmly the outpouring of rage meant to confuse you just as it did when you were a child. If in the heat of the moment you waver ever so slightly, you will find yourself returning to your old status of infant victim, answering injustice with resentment, a resentment so full-blown now that it may even tempt you to suicide or parenticide.

Rest assured, "they" know all the buttons to press, because "they" created them in you, and you have kept them oiled and ready by means of your resentment and self-righteous judgments. And since they created you, they feel they have a right to destroy you. If that is the case, you are no longer dealing with parents, but with a displaced identity, a netherworld personality that goads you to hate in order to continue living through you.

Therefore, don't be too surprised should your candor be rejected, and you find yourself cast out, disinherited, and accused of being the ungrateful offspring of the most wonderful, caring parents in the world. "They" (in quotes because we are not speaking here of their original identity, but of the evil spirit that has taken possession of them) will try to make you think you have committed the unforgivable sin against "god," for which you must one day come crawling on your knees, begging forgiveness. Indeed, resentment toward a parent *is* a sin against God; so the trick is to induce you to become hateful toward them so that the thing inside your parents can enslave you into making up to them forevermore.

If, on the other hand, you don't take the bait and you remain calm and unmoved by their display of anger and violence, you may see a sudden shift in their tactics, a pantomime of false remorse, a dramatic charade of sorrow. Behold a cowering parent "wickedly betrayed" by the child to whom she has devoted her whole life. Careful, "it" is trying to play on your sympathy, seeking to capitalize on any resentment-based guilt that may still linger inside you. Fall for this ploy, be moved by it to the slightest degree, and you will be drawn so deeply into a black vortex of doubt that you will be glad to suffer endless servitude in an effort to atone for the sin of hate; yet you can never find salvation through the hard-won approval of another person. That way leads only to greater anxiety of self-condemnation.

Your memories are yours alone and you are stuck with them. Don't expect your parents to remember a thing. They were cruel and thoughtless toward you because they themselves were abused as children, and through hating their parents, they became the parents they hated. Then, because they couldn't bear to face what they had become, they chose the classic way to block out their guilt: they projected the wickedness inside themselves into you. They did unto you unconsciously what had been done unto them. From that point on, they stayed busy being angry with the wrong they had implanted in you, thus distracting themselves from the guilty knowledge of their own part in it. Of course, anger was the means by which they "got" to you in the first place, so be careful with their rage. They are still trying, albeit unconsciously, to project their guilt into you and take on your innocence in a macabre kind of trade.

Once the guilty exchange is made between the generations, the mechanism of denial will lock in for you, even as it did for them, and you will grow to become a "conscienceless" violator of your own little children. You, too, will be unable to see why you have problems with them. Your awareness will be dulled by the subtle mechanism of anger/denial. You may not see what you are doing, or you may not realize that what you are doing is the cause of the problem.

Children always seem to be the problem, but they are merely victims of their environment, helpless in their undeveloped state of consciousness to speak up and neutralize their parents' madness. Surely you remember the tongue-tied helplessness you felt many times when faced with grown-up injustice. You saw it so clearly; yet you were unable to find words to reach the ears of your tormentors. So you shut up, and grew a shell of self-righteousness over your resentment.

Now, as an adult, you must approach your guilt-ridden

parents with calmness and wisdom; but in order to do so, you must already have forgiven them and arrived at a state of grace, so that it is the real *you* confronting them, full of understanding, a stranger to emotional judgments. Should you react as you did when you were a child, with overt or masked resentment, the magic of the moment will be lost. The real parent and real child will never come to know each other. Instead, the iron doors of contempt, hatred, guilt, and guilt-based servitude will clang shut between you. You will be tormented by the awareness of the indwelling image of the hated parent who is living his life through you. Your hate will drive you to appease this parental ghost, even after he or she has gone to the grave. You may even become worse than your parents ever were, hurting your children, punished by the full knowledge of what you are doing, yet unable to stop.

Remember, resentment is the heartbeat, the blueprint of the self you loathe, even as you continue to sustain it with each prideful "fix" of judgment. In the absence of mature poise and patient understanding, the reaction associated with a parent/child confrontation could become your *permanent* guilt and undoing. It will affect every area of your life.

Your failure to deal properly with your parents will be duplicated many times over in your dealings with authority figures of all kinds. Many alcoholics got started by turning to the bottle to take out their frustration with the unjust bureaucracy at city hall. Parents, school teachers, and bureaucrats of all sorts, have, more often than not, capitulated to the system and have thereby become what they hated in their own lives. You must realize that their defense is to get completely absorbed in their role. The truth of a little child challenges them to reject it wherever and in whomever it appears. So does the beast protect its guilty ego from being awakened by the protestations of the innocent.

Your objective, then, should be to mend fences, to give your father, mother—bureaucrats too—the opportunity to see the harm they are doing. They must be persuaded to come to repentance, not only for their own salvation, but also for the future of their children and grandchildren. But until you have suffered sufficiently from the "weakedness" of your father and the subtle, or overt, "wickedness" of your mother—until you can stand in their shoes—you cannot really perceive any secret torment they may be suffering. Their torment is your torment, and their shoes are your shoes. For God's sake, don't go on becoming them by hating them. Forgive them, and let that forgiveness act as a mirror to their sin.

Forgiveness erases past memories. To forgive is to forget, to clear the slate. The fool just tries to forget, to blot out guilt by distraction. And you have been that distraction. As such, you now place yourself in danger by jogging your parents' memory with the contrast of your recaptured innocence.

Denial is salvation to the sinning soul. The longer a person exists while denying truth in one way or another, the more wicked he becomes, and the greater grows his need to deny. For the ego-self to survive in this state, it must go on denying; and the selfishness of this is so horrible that it drives to distraction all those who try to awaken him.

For whatever goodness is still alive in your tormentors, your love is their only chance, their mirror. Be patient.

Don't waver, or you will be forever tied to their hell.

And why should you give them a chance? Because you now know what love is. Hate has always tricked you, kept you from infilling love. Pain has made you restless, and searching has brought you to the threshold of compassion. Perhaps, as with you, there still is a little child imprisoned in them by their private demon. Someone must give them a chance to see and be set free. Who shall it be? Who is bold enough, close enough—who knows and cares enough—other than you? The responsibility is yours. Come forward now. Face the fury. Be the matador with the bull.

You have suffered and searched, and you have found within yourself the love you were denied from without. You hated, and were therefore denied love. You became the hate thing that separated you from love; which, standing unholy in the place of the holy, separates your own children from love and innocence, and separates you from God's love. You have the gift, the power now to give up hate and to return your parents to love.

It is right that parents be good to their children, for such goodness breeds respect for parents, and helps the children to become receptive to sound teaching; which is, to love and not fall into the abyss of hate.

Despair not. The love you were denied through hating your parents' failures and/or their cruelty can be found in another way. Through suffering, you have discovered that hatred for parents (especially for a father) is a denial of God's love. So when you finally allow yourself to see the truth of this (if only because you stand helpless in your parents' shoes), your heart will be softened by revelation; and through forgiving your father/mother will you be forgiven; and with forgiveness will you approach your parents again.

You see, the love of a loving father does not originate from the man himself, but from his allegiance to the same source of love as the one that resides in you and perceives respect and love within him. Sadly, few fathers have this loyalty to good. Their heritage is like your own. An evil sprang up and made a home in them through their mothers, who tricked them into hating their fallen fathers; and consequently, they too were blocked, no matter how much they may have tried to love you properly.

Let us remember a famous son's last words: "Forgive them, Father, for they know not what they do." Then, as now, some of the people's hearts were opened, while others died miserably in their sins.

Most of us are the sum total of our experiences, but another way of saying this is that we are burdened down and bothered by our past. Unless we learn to respond properly in the present moment, the present becomes merely an extension of that burdensome past.

Roy Masters, author of this persuasive self-help book, describes a remarkably simple technique to help us face life properly, calmly. He shows us that it is the way we respond emotionally to pressures that makes us sick and depressed.

By leading us back to our center of dignity and understanding and showing us how to apply one simple principle, Roy Masters shows us how to remain sane, poised and tranquil under the most severe trials and tribulations.

Roy Masters has nothing less to offer you than the secret of life itself—how to get close to yourself and find your lost identity, the true self you have lost in the confusion.

The observation exercise materials consist of the book, *How Your Mind Can Keep You Well,* and three (3) cassettes of the same title. We suggest a donation of $30, or whatever you can afford.

New Dimensions

New Dimensions is a magazine dedicated to helping you understand and deal with the problems and pressures of everyday life. Each issue of *New Dimensions* presents eye-opening insights into familiar and difficult personal and family problems such as: sex, love, anxiety, bad habits, disease, and death. *New Dimensions* leaves no subject untouched, attempting to expose and dispel the misconceptions that plague our modern society. Perhaps the most accurate description of this fast-growing publication would be: *a mind-expanding resource of insights, new ideas, and spiritually uplifting information that stimulates higher thinking and positive action.*

You will receive 12 monthly issues, each containing information and articles that could change your life and save you thousands of dollars by providing you with provocative answers to problems doctors and psychiatrists haven't even begun to understand.

To subscribe to *New Dimensions* write: The Foundation of Human Understanding, P.O. Box 34036, Los Angeles, CA 90034, or P.O. Box 811, Grants Pass, OR 97526.

Subscription rates:

U.S.: one year $36 third class; two years $66. One year $48 first class; two years $90. Foreign: one year $52 surface; two years $98. One year $78 A.O. Air; two years $150.

LISTEN TO THE PROGRAM

"How Your Mind Can Keep You Well"

A live radio program with Roy Masters

Roy Masters hosts a live call-in program every morning Monday through Friday from 9:00 a.m. to 9:30 a.m. on radio station KIEV*, and 9:30 a.m. to 10:00 a.m. on radio station KTYM*, both originating from Los Angeles. After the live program, he continues to take calls off the air from 10:00 a.m. to 11:00 a.m. These shows will be aired at a future date.

On the program, Roy answers questions on every topic concerning the human condition, helping people to look at their problems from an objective point of view. Roy's program and entire organization are sponsored by donations from his listening audience and people who have gained benefit from his teachings.

Some stations reach areas not described below. For specific information on stations that you may be able to receive in your city or in different parts of the country, call the Foundation of Human Understanding at (213) 559-3711.

*KIEV and *KTYM live call-in programs.
Local: (213) 559-3712
Long Distance: (213) 559-3716

MEDITATION PACKAGE

"How Your Mind Can Keep You Well"

Instruction in the basic technique of meditation as taught by Roy Masters. Consists of three compact cassettes and a book by the same name. $30

If you cannot afford the price of the basic meditation materials, it is the policy of the Foundation to allow you to pay what you can afford. Please be fair.

BOOKS

1. How Your Mind Can Keep You Well
2. How to Control Your Emotions
3. How to Conquer Suffering Without Doctors
4. The Secret of Life
5. Sex, Sin & Salvation
6. No One Has to Die
7. The Satan Principle
8. Healers, Gurus & Spiritual Guides
   (by William Wolff)
9. How to Survive Your Parents
10. The Adam & Eve Sindrome

All books listed above are $7.95 ea.

LECTURES ON . . .

MEDITATION

Basics of Meditation (#1160) 90 min./$10
The Key to Meditation (#1961) 90 min./$10
Advanced Techniques of Meditation
(#1176) 90 min./$10
Is Meditation for Christians? (#1944 1 & 2) 120 min./$12

ROY MASTERS SPEAKS

Man-Woman Relations, Part 1 (#1371) 60 min./$10
Man-Woman Relations, Part 2 (#1786) 90 min./$10
Man-Woman Relations, Part 3 (#1840) 90 min./$10
Man-Woman Relations, Part 4 (#2615) 90 min./$10
Man-Woman Relations, Part 5 (#2807) 90 min./$10
Man-Woman Relations, Part 6 (#4187) 90 min./$10
Man-Woman Relations, Part 7 (#4373) 90 min./$10
Resolving Family Problems (#1388) 90 min./$10
The Power of Words (#1399) 90 min./$10
Why Children Have Problems (#1410) 90 min./$10
Injustice (#1413) 90 min./$10
Dealing Properly With Children (#1441) 90 min./$10
The Effects of Music (#1525) 90 min./$10
The Meaning of Faith (#1599) 90 min./$10
False Belief (#1605) 90 min./$10
The Power of Realization (#1608) 90 min./$10
Understanding the Lower Self (#1699) 90 min./$10
Pride, the Cause of Death (#1750) 90 min./$10
All About Judgment (#2351) 90 min./$10
So You Don't Think There's a Devil, Eh?
(#2423) 65 min./$10
Homosexuality: The Cause (#2443) 90 min./$10
Overcoming Overeating (#2464) 90 min./$10
Tyrants & Wimps (#2596) 90 min./$10
Willfulness (#2665) 90 min./$10
Understanding Failure: The Key to Success
(#2699) 90 min.$10
Confusing Women, Confounded Men
(#2719) 90 min./$10
Friends, Family & Speaking Up (#2737) 90 min./$10
Vanity (#2817) 90 min./$10 (Formerly 11/84 T.O.M.)
Doubt, Insecurity and Starting Your Own Business
(#2903) 90 min./$10
Guiding Children With Common Sense
(#2947) 90 min./$10
How to Give Up Smoking (#2991) 90 min./$10
Male Sexuality (#2993 1 & 2) 180 min./$20
Female Sexuality (#2995 1 & 2) 180 min./$20
Diseases of Resentment (#3083 1 & 2) 180 min./$20
Roy Masters Talks to Kids (#4169) 90 min./$10
Learning to Live Without Worry (#4297) 90 min./$10

HEALTH

Healing (#1682) 90 min./$10
Faith Healing (#2030 1 & 2) 130 min./$12
Faith & Hope (#1875) 90 min./$10
Sickness & Disease (#1220) 90 min./$10
Cancer & Heart Attacks (#1602) 90 min./$10
Death & Dying—Life & Living
  (#1112-1113) 120 min./$12
Alcoholism: The Cause and Cure (#2575) 60 min./$10
Food, Damnation & Salvation
  (#2835 1 & 2) 180 min./$20

RELIGION

Finding God (#2140) 60 min./$10
Be Still & Know (#1601 1 & 2) 120 min./$12
Beyond Knowlege (#1510 1 & 2) 180 min./$20
Secret Path to the Paradise State
  (#1116 1 & 2) 120 min./$12
Creation vs. Evolution (#2252) 90 min./$10
Overcoming Evil (#2256) 90 min./$10
What it Really Means to Conquer Evil
  (#2452) 90 min./$10
The Crisis of Faith & Doubt (#2633) 90 min./$10
Antidote to Original Sin (#3053) 90 min./$10
How Evil Begins and Ends (#3065 1 & 2) 120 min./$12
The Sins of the Fathers (#4021) 90 min./$10
Finding the Teacher Within (#4271) 90 min./$10

SUCCESS & SURVIVAL

How to Win an Argument (#4357) 90 min./$10
How to Solve All Your Problems
  (#4234) 140 min./$16
Violence in the Family and Nation
  (#4270) 90 min./$10
What is Destroying America (#4088) 90 min./$10
How to Survive in a Society Gone Crazy
  (#4029) 90 min./$10
Moral & Financial Survival (#2131) 60 min./$10
Success Without Ambition (#1921) 90 min./$10
Success Without Destruction (#1922) 90 min./$10
Success Without Guilt (#4321) 90 min./$10

SPECIAL SEMINARS

Hypnosis of Life—Oregon '81
  (#1905 1 & 2) 180 min./$20
Hypnosis of Life—Boston '84
  (#2853 1, 2, 3, & 4) 360 min./$36
Hypnosis of Life—San Francisco '85
  (#2948 1, 2, 3, & 4) 360 min./$36

EMOTIONAL PROBLEMS

Understanding Emotions (#1240) 90 min./$10
Emotional Blocks (#1888) 90 min./$10
The Secrets of Dealing With Stress
  (#2196) 90 min./$10
Happiness (#1883) 90 min./$10
Bad Habits (#1375) 90 min./$10
Psychic Vampirism (#1705) 90 min./$10
The Truth About Sex (#2112) 90 min./$10
Sex & Violence—Love & Hate (#1188) 90 min./$10
Addiction to Drugs, Sex & Alcohol (#1962) 90 min./$10
The Dangers of Music (#2195) David Masters 90 min./$10
Dominance & Subservience (#2048) 60 min./$10
Identity—Uncovering the True Self
  (#1960) 90 min./$10
Conquering the Suggestive Power of Words
  (#1500 1 & 2) 180 min./$20
Secrets of Salvation (#1270) 90 min./$10
Marriage: It Doesn't Have to Be a Living Hell
  (#2315) 90 min./$10
Bigotry (#2369) 90 min./$10
Selfishness (#2397) 90 min./$10
Change Your Attitude—Change Your Destiny
  (#2629 1 & 2) 120 min./$12
Dealing With Wicked Authority (#2631) 90 min./$10
A Deeper Look Into Family Problems
  (#2557) 90 min./$10
Becoming Perfect (#2767) 90 min./$10
The Blessings and Benefits of a Poor Memory
  (#2822) 90 min./$10
Revenge and Forgiveness (#2823) 120 min./$12
You Don't Have to Be Ruled by Inferior Beings
  (#2929) 90 min./$10
Resolving Past Sins (#2939) 90 min./$10
Seeking the Blessed State of Mind
  (#2975) 90 min./$10
Forgiveness (#3069) 90 min./$10
Understanding the Subconscious Mind
  (#4381) 90 min./$10

POSTAGE

Please include $1.30 per cassette or book for third class postage; $1.75 for cassette or $2.50 for book, first class. When ordering materials please send your check or money order to:

The Foundation of Human Understanding
P.O. Box 34036
Los Angeles, CA 90034